I AM a Brilliant Woman

Volume Three:

Stories of women who have taken off their
masks to reveal their true selves

Karen Klassen

Contributing Authors

Kelly Dreisinger

Jane Zakreski

Filomena May

Florence Shustack

Gina Papanou

Trina Rowsell

Joanne Neweduk

Brianna Hallet

Brandi Taylor

Tessa Labbe

Althea Powell

Tai-Monique Kristjansen

I AM a Brilliant Woman Volume Three

Copyright © 2018 by Imagine Seminars Publishing

(A Division of Imagine Seminars Inc.)

Editor: I. Leona Davis

Cover Design by Panagiotis Lampridis

For inquiries, please contact: Karen Klassen

www.womenembracingbrilliance.com

ISBN: 978-0-9918890-4-4

First Edition

Table of Contents

This book is dedicated to the courageous women who are awakening and reclaiming their feminine power and the men who honour them.

Introduction

Brilliance: radiating a high degree of light.

The women's stories you are about to read will remind you that in taking off your mask you set yourself free.

Most of us can recall memories when we were a young girl and someone we trusted with our secrets betrayed that trust. Maybe you were laughed at, teased or ridiculed. Any time we feel hurt it can cut like a knife and if it happens over and over again we tend to put walls up to hide our hurt, our anger or our sadness.

This is how our mask is unconsciously created and reinforced. And we may wear the mask for many years, sometimes never taking if off. In the process of hiding ourselves behind our mask we can forget who we really are. We often wear a mask as it connects to one of our deepest fears, the fear of being rejected.

The mask itself is a metaphor for hiding our unresolved pain behind a protective wall that we have built around our heart – we then refuse to show our authentic self. We may think that we are protecting ourselves from pain and at the same time we are also hiding from the love, joy and fulfillment that we are seeking.

There are many masks women can wear. There is the mask that hides their darkest secrets and there are masks that hide their brilliance for fear of being seen as too happy, too successful or too bright.

I get it! When I began the journey of taking off my masks, I remember sharing my new-found spiritual beliefs and dreams with my girlfriends only to be made fun of. I have shared my insecurities with people who have in turn used them against me. I have reached out in friendship only to be rejected. For many years I wore the mask of normality – hiding my light and downplaying my successes.

I realized that taking off the mask meant being honest with myself. Being truthful in what I needed, what I wanted and what my heart desired shifted my reality in profound ways. I no longer needed trauma, drama or tragedy to motivate me to spiral up in life. I was done hiding behind my addictions, hiding behind the men in my life and hiding behind my fears of what others would think about me as I pursued my goals and dreams.

This book reminds us how we always want to put our best face forward as we want our friends, our family and the people we meet to think highly of us. Yet, in order for someone to truly know you they must know your extremes – your fears and your passions. I feel the best way to know someone is through their story; to know where they have been and how they became the person they are today.

However, letting others in to see the inside of you before you have seen the inside of you can cause emotional pain and suffering to rise to the surface. It can hurt especially when you have yet to discover your own inner brilliance.

Taking off the mask is a journey of self-discovery. For you to truly know yourself, you must know your extremes – your dark and your light. To the degree you experience the darkest of your own emotions is to the degree to which you can experience the highest expression of your light.

If you have yet to take off your masks, I invite you to begin by writing in a journal. Write your own story; the hurts, the wounds, and then reflect on how each of these experiences were divinely designed to empower you to take off your own masks. Be patient and have compassion for yourself as you awaken to your own true identity.

Be willing to risk being vulnerable. Seek support from those who have had the courage to take off their masks whether that is a trusted friend, a women's circle, a therapist or spiritual coach who has loving acceptance, a compassionate ear and an understanding of where you are. For only those who have been there can truly understand.

If we never let anyone know that we are having difficulty with something, we deny the possibility of guidance and we deny other women the opportunity to be encouraged by our own challenges.

This book is Volume Three of the, *I AM a Brilliant Woman* series, and it is an invitation for women around the world to stand in their power. To unapologetically declare, "I AM a Brilliant Woman" no matter what they have been through!

In the pages ahead are twelve women who have courageously taken off their masks to reveal their true selves. They have contributed their stories and in doing so, they each offer you a glimpse into their lives and the journey they took from fear to love, from hurt to healed and from shame to truth revealed.

The time is now for all of us to shine our inner *brilliance*.

Together We Rise!

Karen Klassen

Founder of Women Embracing Brilliance

The Brilliant Woman Declaration

I (your name) make a heart centered commitment that from this moment forward, I will never degrade, gossip, cut down, or say mean or spiteful words to or about another woman. She is my sister and is a reflection of who I am. I love myself way too much to speak negatively about others.

And so it is.

I AM Resilient

Divine Storm

By Kelly Dreisinger

This story is an example of how the universe shakes up a person's life when… shall we say… a "course correction" is needed. The circumstances that led to and caused the devastation in my life… and my resilient journey of rising above and recovering a new life!

Let me introduce you to the antagonist of my story...

The Con Artist

You came into my life like a knight in shining armour. I had no idea, of the carnage in harbour.

I was a sucker for your charm. I never even considered that you would bring me harm.

You dazzled with excitement just like a Rock Star! The power of your promises, made my fantasies go far.

But you are a predator and I am your prey. You are the glutton, at MY buffet.

A wolf in sheep's clothing, you were clad. I was naïve... gave you everything I had.

You used and abused my trusting heart. Fraud was your goal, right from the start.

You and your cronies were slick with greed. Like poisonous snakes, with intent to deceive.

You took my money, and my freedom was dashed. My lifestyle is gone, my dreams have crashed.

I gave you the benefit of the doubt, one too many times. Now I'm paying the price, for your unethical crimes.

You're nothing but a con man, who took me for a ride. How do you sleep at night, with your morals and lies?

You brought me to my knees and rocked me to my core. Stripped me emotionally, left sobbing on the floor.

And now you have the audacity, to deny you've done wrong?! Where are your ethics, you freaking moron?

How is this okay... in your mind? I hope that karma takes care of your kind.

I can't imagine your family being proud. Of the man you are and the destruction you plowed.

Someday you will face and answer to God. Why you committed, theft and fraud.

It's a bitter pill to swallow, the legacy of your con. But for my own sake, I am moving on.

And thank God I'm strong, as strong as I need! To rise above your deception and greed.

The day that I met JC, the *con artist*, was the day that my life changed forever… I just didn't know it yet. At that time, I was a wealthy divorcee. I was also extremely naïve and vulnerable. JC was an arrogant, greedy and unscrupulous investment advisor with inadequate experience… Our partnership was a recipe for disaster. In one year, two-thirds of my wealth had been swindled away by the extravagant promises of riches coming my way by the 'lucrative investments' he presented. I believed him… hook, line and sinker. Why? A few reasons… and there was a lot going on behind the scenes that came into play.

Firstly, there was a lawyer present and involved in the transactions, so that gave me the comfort level that all was well. Secondly, I had no financial management experience or knowledge at all. My ex-husband handled that end of things. I didn't have a clue about investments, so I was gullible. Also, my nature is a trusting and kind soul that seeks approval and acceptance from others, so it was easy for JC to manipulate me because I did not have the knowledge to discern otherwise. He asserted himself as an authority figure, assured me that he would not put me in anything of a high-risk nature and that he was being diligent.

He also convinced me that my other substantial investments that I held overseas were crashing and that I had better get out of them before I lost it all. Unfortunately, getting out of them early cost me dearly, but he was okay with that as I could then invest that money into 'his' investments... that were structured to make him money.

Before all this happened, I had been married to a wonderful man for twenty-five years. We met when I was nineteen, and he was fresh out of university with an engineering degree. I was a carhop at the local burger joint. Everyone, including myself, thought that I was so lucky to 'catch' him. As his career took off, we were afforded with the material displays of success. We lived in nice houses, traveled the world and lived internationally. I felt lucky to be a stay at home mom for our three children because I had grown up the opposite way, in a single mother household, and did not want that for my children or self.

Unfortunately, my husband and I did not have the communication skills or emotional maturity to navigate the sometimes choppy waters of life, marriage, parenthood or our personal and intimate relationship. We were drifting apart and we both avoided and withdrew rather than manage our relationship with loving care. I used alcohol as an escape... and as a way to numb my feelings… as I had been doing since I was a teenager. I was living behind the 'everything is wonderful' mask, but I was dying inside.

We lost each other, and I lost myself. I felt as if I was the infection, and the only way to make everything better was to get rid of the infection, right? I left the marriage and the self-destruct button had been pressed.

From the outside looking in, I had an extraordinary life of fun and adventure. I traveled the world whenever I wanted; I did not need to work and did not have any financial worries at all.

But on the inside, I was operating on a lifestyle of alcohol abuse, limiting beliefs and a raging ego. My life was out of balance and my inner compass was off because I was living a lifestyle that was not conducive to making fully aware and grounded decisions. My ego compelled me to make poor decisions because I wanted to earn my 'own' money and be successful in my 'own' right, because my wounded inner child did not fully believe that I deserved that money… and that I was not worthy of it. And because of those beliefs… boom… universe took care of that by bringing this person in to my life.

I wasn't paying enough attention to the financial aspect of my life, because I trusted JC fully and believed that he was managing things appropriately… because he led me to believe that he was.

You see, con artists have an uncanny ability to tell you what you need to hear in order to feel safe and secure. That is how they are so successful in their manipulations.

By the time I realized that something was not right…everything was wrong. All the money that I had invested was gone. An amount large enough that some people would slit their wrists over. My money had vanished into Ponzi schemes, bad investments and unbeknownst to me, supporting his lifestyle.

I couldn't believe it. I didn't want to believe it. "How could that be?! What do you mean my money is gone… like, forever?! Those investments would come around, wouldn't they?"

No… they would not.

This reality was a life-altering trauma. My whole foundation… my security blanket… my comfort zone… was gone. The horror of this realization overwhelmed me.

I've come to realize that every life-altering trauma, no matter what that trauma is, results in an emotional destruction and then a process of recovery. I've had to work through the stages of loss and grief just like anyone that has suffered a crippling loss.

I lost my trust… in others and mostly in myself. I questioned why and how could this happen? How can I ever trust myself again or anyone else for that matter? I lost my confidence. I did not have a career to fall back on; I didn't even have a resume. I was 50 years old with little work experience and now had no retirement. The panic set in. My self-esteem was shattered. It felt like my life had blown up along with my mind. The fear was paralyzing.

I drew inward for a couple of years in order to process what had happened. For a while, I needed to wallow in despair and self-pity. I realized that I had held a belief that I needed someone to take care of me financially... that I was not capable on my own. I believed that I was not smart enough or good enough. I wallowed in the question of, *what will I do?*

You can't imagine the pain unless you've experienced it yourself. My money, material possessions, my affluent lifestyle and my retirement are gone. I suffered deep emotional and mental trauma as my reality had been changed forever. My whole sense of feeling safe and secure in this world had vanished. The security that gave me a foundation... a belonging... a future, had been taken away. Losing this safety net drove me to despair, where I felt unhinged and fearful. I felt the pain of betrayal on so many levels.

On the personal side, JC nurtured a fun and friendly relationship with frequent talks, texts and business lunches that kept up the buzz about all the exciting possibilities he was working on, and all the great opportunities for me... both professionally and financially. On the professional side... he lied to me from our very first meeting, and continued to lie throughout the whole relationship. He told me that he was licensed and insured… he wasn't. He told me so many things, that I have since found out the truth about. I realize now that when we met, he probably thought that he had struck gold with me and I was his 'cash cow'. He was trying to use my money to make himself rich.

With all that had occurred and the resulting situation, I also got to experience intense anger. That took a while to surface for me because I first had to move through the shame and embarrassment. When I think about this experience, there is still anger that rises up. I acknowledge this feeling and at the same time, I know I am personally accountable for what happened.

As I was spinning with the overwhelming circumstances of my reality, as well as the lawsuits, I realized that I was at a crossroads in my life. I could either allow this life-altering event to get the best of me, and spiral down into a boozy gutter, or rise above. Thank God, my spirit was strong enough to know that the first choice was not an option, as I was already on my recovery journey. I decided to face the situation and dug in for the fight of my life.

My healing became my priority. I surrounded myself with family and friends to support me. I took in counseling, coaching, a variety of healing modalities and made the effort to connect with heart centered women in order to move forward.

Seemingly all of a sudden, I was gifted with what I can only describe as a divine expression. My soul just started pouring out of me in the form of poetry. I had tapped in to my truth, into my inner brilliance, and she was setting me free. Each word, and each tear shed, was a healing balm to my soul. I became absorbed with my writing. Over the next few weeks and months, I penned many poems that chronicled my healing as this next poem expresses...

My Pieces

My life as I knew it was blown to shreds. The pieces scattered like wind-blown threads.

This divine storm tore me apart. My self-esteem shredded, a gaping hole in my heart.

Without my foundation, my values were crossed. Who was I now? My spirit was lost.

"How did this happen?" and "Why me?" I cried. It was time for my comfort zone, to be brushed aside.

I plunged down, into depths of despair. I had to surrender and cry out in prayer.

For the lessons in life, that I needed to discover. My inner strength and faith in God to uncover.

I soon realized there was a choice to make. Let myself go... or rise up for my own sake.

My spirit dug in and would not let me crash. I will overcome, and mend the gash.

My path to freedom is a healing journey. To put back the pieces that are meaningful to me.

Living in balance… with integrity. Choosing faith and trust, brings me serenity.

I'm uncovering my strengths that I did not see. I'm finding pride… as I discover me.

But letting go and shedding the mask. Being authentic is no easy task.

The trauma cut deep, I have a mountain to climb. To put back my life… one piece at a time.

My poems were the beginning of my spiritual and personal growth. Now I see that this whole 'divine storm' of my life had to happen. Not TO me, but rather, FOR me. It was my universal smack-down to wake me up and strive to become the brilliant woman that I truly am.

Firstly, I had to embrace and accept what had happened in order to move on. Yes, I was taken advantage of and the lessons I've learned from that are invaluable. I have had to, and continue to, confront my inner demons… my limiting beliefs, self-doubt, fears, attitude and lifestyle.

Now, I know what it means to do our 'inner work' in order to create the life we want. I am thankful for the empowered growth of my journey and the many gifts that I am receiving because of it. Every day, I strive to make the choice to accept and love myself. Some days are easier than others.

Lastly, I choose to have faith that everything will be okay. I believe that with desire and intention, hope, faith and mindfully inspired action towards a positive outcome, the universe will respond likewise.

Life goes on. I am healing and growing as I am getting to know the new me. I am moving forward on this journey and not allowing this experience to hold me back in becoming the woman I am meant to be.

About Kelly

While reeling in the depths of a traumatic life change, Kelly was gifted with divine expression in the form of poetry. In the midst of her heartache, this greatest gift assisted in her healing journey, and rising above those circumstances.

Kelly's poems tell a story that takes the reader on a vivid journey. She dives deep into addiction and recovery, feelings and fears, struggles and triumph, relationships and life.

This period in her life forced Kelly to wake up and take back control of her life in a wonderful and positive way while uncovering her strengths, resilience and path to loving herself. In doing so for herself, Kelly's inspiring poems may empower other women around the world that are perhaps struggling with similar issues.

Finding her voice through her poems has given Kelly a purpose and a passion. She understands that her poems are to be shared with the women of the world through books, videos and songs. Kelly is currently creating an exciting new business in order to share this purpose.

You may connect with Kelly at www.kellydreisinger.com.

I AM a brilliant woman because I am rising above my circumstances to become the brilliant woman that I am meant to be!

– Kelly Dreisinger

I AM Powerful

The 5'1"Financial Powerhouse in Stilettos

By Filomena May

I stood at the doorway. I hesitated. Everyone was wearing black. Remembering who I am as a brilliant woman I knew I was meant to be here. I took a deep breath and exhaled. I walked tall into a sea of men wearing a white dress and my 4" stilettos. I was ready to be the one to stand out in the crowd.

I love being an entrepreneur. I always envisioned myself as a teacher and quickly developed a passion for empowering women around their finances. The investment world is full of sharks and rising through the ranks of ego-driven men who do not respect the feminine has been challenging. There was and still is, a gap in the financial world and I knew it was time for women to take their learning and involvement to the next level and create the financial freedom they desire.

My journey to running my own wealth management office has not been easy; however, looking back at how my parents moved to Canada with little gives me a sense of gratitude. I had the privilege of a decent education so that I could have a "good job" when I grew up. Although being raised as an Italian-Canadian had its challenges.

I was bullied regularly in school. I was not able to wear the trendy fashions, not allowed out much, and eating big bowls of pasta daily certainly didn't help my waistline, so my self-image and self-worth were not good.

Dating as a young woman was not fun as I was given strict rules. My parents are strong Catholics and believe in no sex until after marriage. I was prohibited from moving out until I was married. I felt as though I was locked up in a jail cell, unable to experience all the things my friends were experiencing.

My parents put me through university and wanted the best life for me and at the same time, this lack of freedom to become independent and think for myself became my own worst enemy. What I realized much later in life is that these childhood experiences would develop into a fear of rejection and abandonment that stuck with me into adulthood.

First year of University was interesting. I drove across town for the first time and went to visit a girlfriend and her brother.

He turned out to be my first promising date who became my husband five years later.

Treat Others The Way You Want To Be Treated

Meeting my husband brought an incredible sense of freedom into my life initially. Six months into marriage at age twenty-two, my husband and I built our first home and purchased a new car. These responsibilities were scary, especially since I had never lived on my own.

On graduation, I had my first taste of male domination working as an engineering co-coordinator at a high-end hotel. Within a year my female manager, whom I felt empowered by, was replaced by a male who voiced that women did not belong in the engineering department. I was harassed daily to the point my hours were reduced in half, but I did not give up. I turned my tears, hurt and humiliation into perseverance and an opportunity for growth.

I found a job posting online and decided to submit my resume to a wealth management firm who called me in for an interview within three weeks. What did I know about money aside from the fact that I needed to save a lot of it? At the age twenty-four, I was told that I would be an optimal candidate as a financial advisor.

My spouse was invited to my final interview and asked if he could handle me being a financial advisor and business owner because most marriages with one partner in this profession end up in divorce. Although, he was very supportive at the time, the resentment built up as I surpassed his income, worked more hours and needed him to do more household duties after our children were born.

The first thing my boss asked me at the time was, "If you had to pick a life quote that you live by, what would it be?"

I responded, "Treat others the way you want to be treated and be true to yourself."

I was excited, nervous and full of fear and at the same time I needed to trust that doors were opening. Besides, I earned such a poor wage at the hotel and felt unfulfilled so I had nothing to lose. Once I accepted the job I was informed my income was 100% commission-based. I also had to build my own clientele and write three exams within a month on investing and insurance of which I knew nothing about. I was so determined to make the next training session that I passed the exams and quit my job at the hotel right away. All the thoughts of not knowing what to expect or how to run a business had me in an anxious state of self-doubt.

Align With People Who Believe in You

First thing my manager had me learn was the financial planning software that most advisors did not know how to use. He said, "To be successful, you need to become a student of the business and be the squeaky wheel; and successful people do what unsuccessful people are unwilling or unable to do." This was the coaching I needed to be tenacious and not give up when things got tough. He definitely tested me on how badly I wanted to succeed. I had to fake it till I made it. I had to sound intelligent and confident while navigating through meetings when he did not show up. I resented my manager for many years but looking back, I thank him for preparing me for the highs and lows, successes and failures, in order to overcome moments of adversity.

One of my biggest obstacles was being taken seriously in the financial world when the average advisor was a sixty-year-old male. There was a 1 in 40 chance of making it in the business, let alone as a young woman.

My first day on the job I was so fearful of being rejected by friends and family that I called people out of the phone book. I was hung up on and sworn at repeatedly, leaving me feeling hopeless. The manager on duty handed me a box of Kleenex, told me that perhaps I wasn't cut out for the business and suggested I quit. I called a mentor who told me to ignore him and keep going. I wiped my tears and said to myself, "I'll show you." Five months later, I won Rookie of the Year.

I decided to create financial plans on the software I learned for the senior advisors. In exchange for the plans and presenting them to clients, I would get a split of the profits or take on the clients into my own practice. This process helped develop my credibility. I also continued my routine of holding seminars, running tradeshow booths and cold calling. I joined weekly training nights at the office, which was designed to be motivational. I then witnessed the same manager that suggested I should quit, watching porn in the bullpen with the other male advisors. That was the end of my evenings with the boys. I chose to motivate myself at home instead. My performance increased and I was recommended for managerial training in order to mentor new advisors. When I announced my pregnancy, that opportunity was no longer available.

My son was born in the midst of the busiest season of the year and I did what it took to ensure my business ran effectively. I had great support from another female advisor and a mother/son team who are friends to this day. They understood motherhood and entrepreneurship first-hand. This gave me the ability to work between naps, diaper changes and feedings.

A couple of years later, I had two defining moments. I gave birth to my daughter and seven weeks later I was in a major car accident. With intense therapy, the love for my children and the passion for my career I was able to stay focused on recovery. I was determined to run and ski again.

I also knew I needed to leave my marriage. I had confirmation when I walked in the house the night of the accident, in pain and an emotional mess, and my husband continued playing his video games as though I had arrived home from grocery shopping.

At the same time, management would not give me new client accounts because they felt I was incapable as a new mother. My intuitive self opened my eyes and told me I was strong enough to step into my feminine power and stand up for who I am as a brilliant woman. Shortly thereafter, I was approached by an independent financial firm and was offered the opportunity to open my own practice… of course, I said YES! It was a big risk knowing I would have to start over but had to trust I was on the right path. Within weeks I was introduced to the owner of a mortgage brokerage and we decided to work together. Business excelled to new levels that I didn't think were possible. He helped me see past my self-limiting beliefs that I wasn't worthy or smart enough to be successful… I was ready to take off the mask and own the truth that I am a 5'1" woman in heels with a lot more power than I thought I had!

Fear as The Double-Edged Sword

I made the choice to end my marriage when my children were four and seven. I knew I had to surrender to the rollercoaster of emotions – fear, shame and guilt – otherwise they would overwhelm me. I knew it was time to move forward and create the life that would allow me to pursue my personal and professional growth to a higher level so I could become my authentic self. I also wanted to be the mother my children would look up to and be of greater service to the community. I came to the realization that life is too short to live the life that others expect me to live.

In the midst of divorce proceedings, I still needed to be proactive with my business as times were changing in the investment world. This meant writing more exams and expanding my practice to one of the top wealth management firms.

I officially moved my company, Filo Financial Solutions, to Raymond James Ltd. I was impressed with their commitment to seeking out female advisors and growing their women's advisory network. In my first year, I was profiled in a corporate video at their National Business Conference. However, I still felt like a minority; less than 10% of the advisors in attendance were women. Most of the time, I was asked whom I worked under. As I hid in the sea of men, my inner insecure voice said, "Am I really supposed to be here?" But I told myself not to give up and instead find my edge.

I was approached by women's empowerment groups that profile female leaders in various industries, to work and collaborate with them. The beginning of my journey was having my first public speaking engagement with PowHerhouse. I would rather die than public speak, but I used fear to fuel me rather than hinder me.

Within the movement of the divine feminine, I felt compelled to deliver a message to women and empower them to find their own unique edge. What I learned is that if we allow others' negative stories and projections of themselves, they can influence our own vision and potential. I realized that I had been self-sabotaging; therefore, slowing down my success with all the naysayers I naively listened too. Although, I practice what I preach financially, success is not just about how much money you make, it is about the difference you create. During a time of weakness and burnout I was able to gain clarity when I looked at life from a bird's-eye view. I focused in and looked at the fine details and then zoomed out to see the bigger picture of how I was going to execute my vision.

I knew I wanted my own branch within five years and it was an 'out there' goal that I wrote down with my executive coach. My dream manifested itself a year later. I had the choice to allow fear to take over or trust that this opportunity presented itself because I was ready for it! My assistant cheered me on and kept me focused.

Although, I try to be superwoman at times, I also knew I needed continued support and would not be where I am without my parents helping raise my children.

Listen To Your Intuition

During the last National Business Conference, I chose to embrace my feminine power and uniqueness that I bring to the financial world. I made the choice to be seen, my vision heard and to stand out in the crowd in my white dress and 4" stilettos. I also felt encouraged knowing that it is not just women that support me; it is also men who have been incredible mentors who believe in me.

The years of negative self-talk where I was "not good enough" were becoming a faded memory. I still catch myself self-sabotaging when I am shifting to the next level of growth, but now I have become more self-aware. The naysayers will always be there to criticize and question what I can handle, but I've realized that perception is not reality and with the ability to listen to my own intuition, I let go of criticism and rejection to remain focused on possibilities. I developed the same mind-set within my community when I recently ran and was elected first female president of my cultural society that began thirty-two years ago.

My intuitive edge is also used to empower my clients. I have helped them navigate through the emotional side of their finances and mentored them. Being able to relate and allow the space to be vulnerable with no judgment has come naturally for me. I take pride in helping women overcome their fear around money… particularly regarding divorce proceedings.

About Filomena

Filomena May is the owner of Filo Financial Solutions of Raymond James Ltd. Raymond James Ltd. is one of the largest independent wealth management firms in Canada. Filomena is also president of the Calgary Calabrese Cultural & Heritage Society. She was born and raised in Calgary, Alberta as a first generation Canadian and is the mother of two children.

Filomena thrives on pushing herself and finding her edge, personally and professionally, so that she can make a positive impact on people as a community leader and an advocate for women's empowerment.

Her intuitive gift and holistic approach has helped many clients build their financial roadmap. She has a passion for helping others see their potential and take action, especially in times of adversity such as divorce.

Filomena can be contacted at

www.raymondjames.ca/filofinancial

I AM a brilliant woman because I use my intuition to empower others to find their edge.

— Filomena May

I AM Blessed

Life with a Purpose

By Althea Powell

As a talk show host on television, I remind people that dreams can come true when we have the courage to believe in ourselves. The path is not easy but so worth it.

In writing about my journey, I trust that I will inspire you to never give up.

For many years, I wore the mask of an angry woman. I have learned how my words and emotions can have either a devastating impact or elevate my children's relationship with me.

My daughter, Daija, my wash belly baby (her name means *my last child*) has felt most of my angry words, words meant for her father but directed at her. I would lose my mind when I was with her father. My behaviour was unbelievable. There came a time when I caught myself and I realized the true impact my words had on the daughter I am supposed to love and protect. To put my trust in a man instead of God was the first mistake I made. I was so disconnected from my soul. I did not know who I was or my purpose in life.

Eventually, I realized that not only was my daughter a princess, she was also a blessing as she saved my life in so many ways. Sometimes, when God brings people into our lives, we need to understand they are there for a purpose. Some come to save, destroy, teach and most importantly, to show us how to love.

I was living a life consumed with hate and anger. It swirled and spiralled, touching everything and everyone around me. When I think of my old self, unhappy and looking for love, I realize I was always searching for love from external sources. Some days I would look in the mirror and I wouldn't see beauty. I'd see a stranger staring back at me so I'd go searching for something material to define who I was.

When I was with my daughter's father, I allowed him to make me feel like I wasn't worthy of love, respect or being treated with decency. After all this, my daughter still worshiped the ground he walked on, so I carried this anger towards him, towards her and most of all towards myself for allowing someone to take so much away from me. I lost the ability to trust those closest to me. I struggled every day to not allow these experiences to diminish my drive.

I grew up in a family of eight, seven sisters and one brother. Crowded doesn't begin to describe my childhood household. In Jamaica, our house was so small that I shared a bed with ten of my cousins. The best part about it was that I didn't think anything of it, to me that was normal. It wasn't until I moved to Canada that I realized that it was not normal.

My mother married an Irishman and they had two children; he became like a father to me. I truly believed he was a good man. However, over time I began to lose the man I thought of as my father. I think it's important to remember that he was caring for eight children and only two belonged to him biologically. The pressure and the demand of being a provider for us started to consume him. There came a time when it was no longer safe for me or my siblings to be around him – not only that, but he was a danger to himself and he had to be taken away. He tried to hurt me and that stuck with me for a long time. Watching someone you love and care for deteriorate into someone unrecognizable can really affect how you love and how you trust. My mother and her husband got an annulment through the Catholic church and after that neither of them were the same. I realize that my mother and stepfather didn't know how to work through their problems.

It took a series of failed relationships before I would even begin to see my inner brilliance. My first husband was addicted to drugs. As you can imagine, a marriage to an addict was the definition of a toxic relationship. He was up, he was down, one minute he loved me and the next he was beating me in front of my son. His erratic behaviour escalated to the point where he burned our house down and threatened the safety of my children. This all occurred before I decided to marry him. The fact that I was willing to marry him speaks to the way I viewed myself. The day I married him, he told me he had to go back to his halfway house and check in. I never saw him again.

These are the things you go through when you're searching for love. I realized that I had not been patient in my quest. That was my issue. I wanted everything immediately and I didn't believe anything better was coming.

On my journey for love and acceptance, a friend shared something. He looked at me and said, "You are such a kind-hearted and beautiful soul. I feel like it's time you found someone to love you unconditionally." He confided in me too that he was ready to marry a woman he had been arranged to marry. He said he didn't want to marry for the physical aspect, he wanted to marry for God. So, he put God first, and through God all things are possible. At first, I did not understand what he meant, how could you marry someone you didn't share a physical, mental or emotional connection with? But now I see that he believed that God would lead him to the right person and I realized that I had to put that out into the universe and wait until God was ready to send someone to me.

It took me a long time to take off the mask and see that I was worth loving and worth waiting for. These realizations came with struggle and experience. I now believe that nothing that is good happens overnight. You must wait, manifest, pray and have faith the size of a mustard seed.

Finally, a new chapter in my life has opened. I feel as though I am in a good place. I did some soul searching trying to heal and learn to forgive and love again. I found a husband, hoping God had picked this one for me and that this time he was the right one. My doubt vanished as soon as I looked into his eyes. I knew he was the one. I listened to my inner brilliance and took my time as my heart was still guarded. I protected my secrets and slowly allowed him to become part of my life.

On my wedding day, I was beautiful. I was stunning. I got married in Jamaica. It was a stressful day because although I knew that I wanted to marry him, memories from the most painful years of my life came flooding back. I began second guessing myself. What if I made a mistake? What if he was just like all the others? My husband waited for me for three hours because I was so afraid of making the wrong choice.

I felt overwhelmed, excited, scared when my son came and looked at me. He said, "Mom, you are the most beautiful woman I have ever seen and it would be my honour to give you away." Everything slowly fell into place and I knew I was exactly where I needed to be and everything I had been through was preparing me for that moment. I was beyond happy. My three beautiful daughters were my bridesmaids and they looked absolutely beautiful, and my wash belly was my flower girl. I was the luckiest woman alive. My son and mother gave me away. It's an image I will never forget: my son had my hand, my mother held the tail of my dress and the only word I could have used to describe it was contentment.

I trembled as I walked to Mr. Odean Powell. Nearly halfway down the aisle I froze and stared at the man that was to be my husband. Against the protocol, against the rehearsal, he walked to me, his hands out, ready to make me his wife. I had tears running down my face; I was so scared that I had ruined my makeup, but through my blurry vision, I saw that he was crying, too.

Reciprocity, (Lauryn Hill put it best in her song *Ex-Factor)* is what I felt on my wedding day – the feeling I've been waiting for – someone who loves me and respects me and cares for me as I do them. In this life, that kind of love can be difficult to find and should be treasured. I knew in that moment I was safe. I knew I made the right choice.

After all, that I've experienced, I realize that life is about making mistakes and learning from them, about using the mistakes to make better choices. When you stop learning, you stop living. Have faith that everything will work out in the end. Faith will take you to that unbelievable place you can turn to when everything else is dark and it feels like there are no more options. I'm still living with faith as small as a mustard seed, but even a little faith is enough – it only takes a little bit of hope.

I've had to fight for everything I have in my life. It didn't come without mistakes and heartbreaks. I genuinely believe that the life I have led has come from God and I know there is a plan for all of us. I find it helpful to think this way. I attempt to live my soul's purpose every day, which is remembering that we come from love. It is not easy, although, the more I choose to love my life, the less I fight it.

I have now landed a talk show on OMNI TV where I am the host. I love it. It is truly my passion. I can reach so many people with my message in a way I never could before. I want to use my life experiences to help others find their paths and if I can save one person from the suffering I have experienced, that's enough. That's why I do my show.

I've found my purpose in life: to embrace people from different backgrounds and empower those who choose to listen to the lessons I've learned in life. And, I am having fun while making a difference. I am looking forward to changing many lives.

I have found what God has made me and that is a brilliant woman, just like every woman out there. All talented, gifted and blessed in many ways and as soon as they realize it, their potential to be great is unparalleled. I'm learning how to make peace with myself, with my insecurities; I'm learning how to accept that I am not perfect and that's okay.

Protecting my children is a lifelong calling. We grow them to be strong, respectful, loving and kind so that they can make this world a better place. I leave you with two very important life lessons so you can pass them on and teach your children how to take their masks off and keep rising up.

One: Love Yourself First

No one can love anyone else or have anyone truly love them if they don't love themselves first. I am living proof of this. When you love yourself you are more patient; you live a good life and are more kind to others. We forget that happiness and self-worth can only be achieved from within.

Two: Have Faith

Life can be challenging and it is faith that will get you through. Believing in a higher power will give you the strength you need to keep moving forward. You are not alone. I feel stronger and happier because I realized that to live a good life is to live one full with learning from your mistakes, learning to love yourself and having faith in yourself and in God. Each day my faith in God grows and I trust that I will one day inspire my daughters and their children to follow their passions, I am grateful to be alive, to be happy and healthy and to be able to have experienced everything that I have so that I can pass it on to others.

I'd like to thank my mother, my son, my daughters, my family and loving husband, and, most importantly, the Lord for allowing me to be where I am today. I hope to continue on this journey learning more about myself and the world around me.

About Althea

Althea's biggest challenge is with her community. She wishes to end the segregation in her city as well as bring the black community together. She supports and encourages others so that everyone can create a positive atmosphere for people of colour and to empower the community by teaching self-love.

Althea started a Facebook live series, where she talks about the issues concerning everyone. She landed her own show, *Island Tea with Althea,* a television series on OMNI TV. She is passionate about interviewing people in politics.

Althea shares what she has learned and offers it up to anyone who will listen.

I AM a brilliant woman as I'm grateful everyday for the blessings and opportunities that have been laid upon me.

– Althea Powell

I AM Grace

Journey to Self Love

By Gina Papanou

I'm sitting in an open cafe on a beautiful resort in Los Cabos, Mexico, overlooking the Pacific Ocean, watching the palm trees dance and breathing in the ocean air. In this moment, I feel so much gratitude and joy for the life I am living, for my family, my friends and for my health and wellness. It feels like I'm living my dream, yet not too long ago, I was lost in a nightmare.

As women, we are caring, loving and giving, and we try to do it all and be it all for the people we love. I was devoted to my students, friends and family, all of whom I highly valued. I then reached a point where I found myself struggling each day to fulfill my obligations. Eventually, I burned out.

Recovering from burnout took a few years and there were times when I thought my life, as I had known it, was over. During these moments, I remember wanting to give up and surrender to my illness, and even though there were many times when it seemed that I didn't have one ounce of energy left, I somehow managed to muster up the strength to keep going, one moment at a time.

I was raised to do my best and be a high achiever and I grew up to become a perfectionist. I learned to believe that what other people thought of me was important, so, like many other women, I became a people pleaser.

My children were my first priority. I wanted to be there for them as much as a working mom could be, and do my best to give them what they needed, including opportunities I never had. I thought if I could do it all and be it all, that meant I was a good mother. If I just kept pushing myself to get up every morning, the day would unfold and everything would get accomplished. Then by the end of a long, stressful day, I'd pass out in bed from exhaustion, wake up the next morning and go through the motions all over again. At the same time, it became apparent that my marriage wasn't working and, eventually, after twenty-three years, we decided to divorce.

As time went on, I struggled increasingly with my emotions, thoughts and physical wellness. I often felt incredibly irritable, and bottled-up feelings would lead to angry outbursts. I didn't realize at the time that these were symptoms of depression.

I had endured depressive episodes as a teenager and as a new mother; however, the depression I experienced during my divorce was by far the worst. It affected all of my relationships and, more importantly, it affected the relationship I had with myself. My internal dialogue became very negative and full of self-punishment.

It's amazing how we human beings live inside our minds. Until we become aware of our thoughts, we don't realize every thought we think is actually creating our reality and, thus, our future. Our mind trusts what we tell it. Until we become aware, we believe that critical voice in our head. We believe that every thought is the truth, but it isn't. It's just a thought.

Going through the divorce was difficult. As if that wasn't enough, my father was suddenly diagnosed with terminal cancer. I remember being shocked and devastated by the news. I visited my dad in the hospital every day where I was his advocate, keeping him company after work and on the weekends. Sadly, he passed away on Christmas Day, a month after his diagnosis.

The grief of my father's passing magnified the emotional turmoil I was already going through. I started having insomnia and severe loss of appetite, but still I soldiered on and continued teaching.

A few months later, I received word that my uncle had abruptly passed away while on vacation in Europe. We had been close since I was a little girl and the news of his passing hit me really hard.

The stress of the divorce combined with the grief of losing my dad and my uncle led to a breaking point. I lost twenty-five pounds in twelve weeks; for the first time in my life, I started having panic attacks. They were terrifying.

Operating on autopilot, I hadn't even considered that I might need to just stop everything and focus on taking care of myself for a change. I knew there was something terribly wrong. I just didn't know what else to do but keep going.

Finally, after consulting my doctor, it became clear that I had no other choice than to take a leave of absence from work. Once I stopped working, my system crashed. I couldn't get out of bed in the morning. I was constantly in tears, fearful of the next panic attack. It felt like I could die at any moment and I was unable to care for myself or do any of the normal things I used to do.

When I started experiencing suicidal ideations, it was frightening. No matter how hard I tried, I couldn't prevent these awful thoughts of doom and death from taking over my mind. At one point, I became afraid to stay home alone, and I was very fortunate to be able to stay with family and friends for as long as I needed. I felt safer and less anxious having people around me and the panic attacks finally subsided.

I also enlisted the help of professionals like a life coach, a counselor and therapists of different types. I told myself if I ever recovered from this, I would live a full, joy-filled life and do all the things I had ever wanted to do with no holding back. The journey was long and arduous. Finally, I reached the point where

I could eat and sleep again, and where people told me the light had come back into my eyes.

This period of time is what I now refer to as my 'dark night of the soul'. As much as it was excruciating to endure, it was also incredibly transformative. It was also a very confusing time for me because I was receiving different messages from different people.

My therapist helped me evaluate my thoughts and limiting beliefs. I described the suicidal ideations to her which went something like this: "your time is done"; "you've lived your life"; "your life is over"; "it's never going to be good again"; "you can't take this anymore"; "Why are you still here"? These kinds of thoughts have a brainwashing effect on you. You start to believe them and that you should do something to end the pain. Your mind automatically starts coming up with scenarios of how you can do it. The key is to notice the thoughts and realize that you still have a choice.

A couple of weeks later, I received a text from my son telling me the news that Robin Williams had committed suicide. The text said, "Mom please be careful!" It was very sobering news and I realized then how extremely worried my kids were about me. I was stunned that someone like Robin Williams, who seemed so full of joy and laughter, could take his own life. You never really know what a person is going through unless they are vulnerable enough to share their experience, which can make the difference between life and death.

At the same time as I was battling the depression, I also had to fight the stigma around me. People who really cared about me would say things like, "You know, why don't you just go back to work?" or "Why don't you get a different job?" or "You'll feel much better if you have somewhere to go every day" or "Don't be lazy". They meant well, but they didn't understand. How could they?

One therapist told me that there was no such thing as depression – that it was a result of my suppressing my true self and being who I thought others wanted me to be. He went on to say depression was a choice I learned, a choice that I was making to avoid my obligations in life. But why would I have panic attacks? It didn't make sense to me.

Another therapist told me I had a chemical imbalance in my brain and that I needed medication to get well again. I didn't want to go on medication because of the stigma and because I thought I wouldn't be myself anymore. With these different opinions, I found it hard to decide what I should do.

As I was doing my own research about what was happening to me, I came across some brain scans by Dr. Daniel Amen – a psychiatrist from the United States who conducts SPECT scans to see how a patient's brain is physically functioning. The difference between the two brain scans of a healthy brain and a depressed brain were quite striking. The healthy brain was plump and lit up all over in a symmetrical pattern, while the depressed brain was smaller and dark all over except for one small area of light. This scan reminded me of the way I had been feeling. Everything appeared dark and hopeless. This image convinced me that depression was a type of inflammation in the brain that impaired my cognitive function and, thankfully as I was learning, it was treatable.

On my journey to recovery, I tried a wide variety of healing modalities such as EFT, meditation, spiritual retreats, and naturopathic, chiropractic, acupuncture treatments. Some of these were incredibly helpful, while others not so much. The key was that I was not going to give up no matter what.

My appetite for learning increased dramatically and as I became stronger, I started reading books by thought leaders like Dr. Wayne Dyer, Marianne Williamson and Dr. David Hawkins. I noticed a common theme in these books: we are spiritual beings having a human experience. Also, that it was important to be true to yourself and to live and speak your truth. If you took care of yourself first, it didn't mean you were selfish. It meant you were filling up your own cup so you could give freely of the overflow to others. Then you could have the passion and the power to follow your bliss and live your life purpose.

The time came to rebuild my life, to choose positive thoughts that served me and to create new possibilities, knowing that I deserved a life I loved. It was time for a fresh new beginning. I was nervous yet hopeful. I made the choice to focus on the good things in my life. I wanted to look forward to the future and I was very grateful for the love I already had in my life through my family, my friends and all the people who cared about me.

Once I reached this point, it was time to re-evaluate the relationships I had. I knew there were people in my life I needed to let go of while wishing them well. These people had not been helpful or supportive of me and some of them were actually quite toxic to be around. I was now learning how to protect my energy from negativity around me. Facing the possibility of dying had given me newfound courage. There was only one direction to go from there and it was up.

Letting go of the past was crucial. I've heard it said that depression is living in the past and anxiety is living in the future. The only moment we really have is right now. In the present moment, we have the power to make choices and take actions that will create the quality of our future.

It was time to base my thoughts, choices and actions on love and courage. That's what makes the difference. Overcoming your fears helps you grow. It was time for a new purpose and for me to exercise my free will. It was also about having the courage to share my story and to listen to others who are on their own life journeys.

It's also important to practice forgiveness towards yourself and towards others. Like most people, there were things I did that I wasn't proud of or mistakes I made that, in hindsight, could have been avoided. The word forgiveness is "for giving" yourself and other people another chance. Forgiveness is a very healing practice, and its power should never be underestimated.

One of the most important practices I adopted was the practice of keeping a daily gratitude journal. I write down two or three new things each day that I'm grateful for and make sure I don't repeat any that I've already thought of before. This creates new neural pathways in your brain and changes your automatic thoughts so they become more positive and better serving.

My life has done a complete turnaround since my healing journey. I'm not only free to explore and experience joy on my own terms, I have met so many wonderful and empowered people along the way who have given me some incredible hope and inspiration.

Through this experience, I have learned it is vital to love yourself and believe in the person you want to become. I've grown to understand that we are human beings, not human doings. In our society, so much of our self-worth comes from what we do for work. There is nothing wrong with taking the time to enjoy life, to live it full out and fully expressed on your own terms. The only judge that matters is you, so give yourself the acceptance and permission to follow your dreams.

Remember, it is never too late. When you do all this and you take care of your mind, body and spirit you have everything you need to create a life you love!

About Gina

Gina Papanou is a Certified Life Coach, Author and Speaker. She is the founder of Wealthy Sprout Life Coaching, which is a partner of the Healthy Wealthy and Wise Coaching Program. Gina is passionate about life-long learning, health, wellness, spirituality and paying it forward. She learned self-love and self-care through the adversity she experienced in her life.

Gina believes we all have the potential to live our highest and best life. A former stockbroker and educator, Gina is passionate about helping her clients create financial freedom and time freedom so they can make healthy, positive changes in their own lives and help make a difference in the lives of others.

Her coaching business is called Wealthy Sprout Life Coaching because she has experienced the power and the potential for people to cultivate and nurture a life of abundance.

Born in Greece, Gina lives in Toronto and has two adult children. She enjoys time spent in nature, travel, music, reading and advocating for social justice and the planet.

You can connect with Gina at www.wealthysprout.com

I AM a brilliant woman because I rise with more power and grace in the face of adversity

– Gina Papanou

I AM Hope

Finding the Family Meant For Me

By Jane Zakreski

I never expected to look back on that night and say, "I made a decision that changed two lives." It started out as a painfully ordinary and bitterly cold January night in Edmonton. I planned to cocoon at home and spend the evening alone.

I had recently moved into the basement of my house and rented out the top floors. This move was my solution to getting my single and thirty-something finances in order. My daily restaurant dining and shopping habits left me without much financial wiggle room. At thirty-eight, it was time to make some changes.

I was also getting over the ending of another disappointing romantic relationship. Feeling sad and weary, I lay draped over my sofa, zoning out on bad TV, and grazing on junk food. There was nowhere else I wanted to be but on that couch.

And the only company I wanted to keep was with my dog, Sam. Sam was my devoted but poorly trained golden cocker spaniel. I had adopted her on a whim a few years earlier. I found her wandering the aisles of a pet store that was hosting a fundraiser for a rescue shelter. Sam looked just like the Disney dog from "The Lady and the Tramp". It was love at first sight.

Now, laying there nearly comatose on my couch, I detected some faint yellow spots dotting the crème coloured rug. My fresh start in my new quarters was getting pissed upon by my darling, Sam. The New Year was not off to an inspiring start.

Suddenly, a friend's voice thundered through my house. I woke up from my cable TV trance. Those old answering machines would broadcast incoming messages if you didn't pick up. And I was indeed in call screening mode that evening. The person on the other end let me know Lindsey's family was in crisis again and encouraged me to call Lindsey that week.

Lindsey was fifteen years old when I first met her six months earlier through one of her relatives. They shared concerns about Lindsey's chaotic home life and feared for her safety. The previous year I had committed to staying open to Big Sister type opportunities in my community. So, I volunteered to meet with Lindsey, and see if I could offer her any support.

When we first met, Lindsey did not look like the girl I expected to see. I'd conjured up some images based on her family story that didn't match the young girl sitting across the table.

Lindsey was a tiny little thing, with porcelain white skin and huge blue eyes. Her presence registered as petite, but fierce, and very self-possessed. She'd wrap blue cotton fabric around her head into what looked like a headdress. Her demeanour was almost regal – she sat so still. I thought to myself, "What an intriguing young girl."

After our visit was over, we kept chatting on the way out of the coffee shop. Lindsey slowed down her pace, and I could tell there was something she was working herself up to say. I stood there patiently, watching while her blue eyes filled with tears. She stared at me without blinking.

After some time, Lindsey blurted out, "I'm afraid my mom is going to die." I had to think about how to respond. What could I tell her that I knew was true?

I know not every parent who is ill recovers - even when they have children who still need them. Your father can die of a heart attack in his sleep in a hotel room, and your mother can die of cancer in a hospital far away from home.

After our long pause, I looked at Lindsey squarely, and said, "Yes, you're right Lindsey, your mother might die – yes, that could happen. Both my parents died when I was young. My dad died when I was your age, and my mom died when I was twenty-one. It was awful to lose my parents so young. But you know what? I made it through – I'm OK. If your mom dies, you can find your way to be OK, too."

We lingered on those facts. In those moments, our bond was created because I told Lindsey the truth. We walked out of the building together into the fresh air and sunlight. Before we said goodbye I asked, "So – do you want to be my friend?"

Lindsey looked at me directly and quietly said, "OK, sure, we can be friends."

"Good," I said. "I'll call you next week."

Fast-forward six months to that cold January night. The message booming from my answering machine didn't sound urgent. The crisis in Lindsey's family didn't seem any different from the rest. I can't say the information set off alarm bells that foreshadowed what came next.

It was Thursday night. Lindsey and I already had a date planned for the weekend. But, for some reason, I followed the nudge. I got off the couch and called Lindsey. I never thought she'd even pick up the phone.

Lindsey answered on the first couple of rings. The fact she responded so quickly struck me as odd. Lindsey was a notorious call screener and normally didn't return calls. But during our call, Lindsey sounded casual. She didn't say anything that made me guess her world had just imploded. Lindsey didn't tell me about the deal she made with her Creator. About her profound despair. About what she promised she would do if someone didn't come to her rescue that night.

I didn't know that if no one showed up, Lindsey was ready to take her life.

The most important conversation of my life began with a simple exchange, "So, do you want to go out to eat?"

"I guess so," Lindsey said.

"OK. I'll be there in twenty minutes," I said.

I bundled up, got into my frozen car, and headed out to Lindsey's house. When I drove up, I could see a couple of lights on in the dining room. I walked up the steps and waited to hear her dog Charlie's loud bark after I rang the doorbell. Charlie was Lindsey's 110-pound Labrador/German Shepherd constant companion and protector.

When Lindsey greeted me at the door, I noticed the gleam from the hardwood floors - there was not a stick of furniture left in the house. Lindsey invited me in to tour the wreckage. Charlie followed us around as we surveyed the echoing space. I walked through the house stunned. I wasn't yet able to put the pieces together.

After the tour, we walked down the steps and away from the house. When we got in the car, Lindsey told me, "I'm worried about Charlie. He threw up, and he hasn't eaten for a couple of days."

"OK, we'll get Charlie some food after we eat," I said.

Soon, Lindsey sat across from me in our booth in the brightly lit restaurant. I watched her, carefully looking over menu items, and deciding what to order. Suddenly, it hit me like a bolt of lightning. I asked the obvious question, "If Charlie hasn't eaten for two days what have you been eating?" I wasn't prepared for her answer. But I was awake to take it all in.

Abandoned in an empty house with no food and a hungry dog, Lindsey had called social services the night before. Nobody called her back. I looked at her in shock and tried to make it all make sense. I couldn't.

When I had awakened that morning, I had no idea how my world, as I knew it, was about to change forever. I lived a life that looked good on paper. But I was still searching for my purpose, for where I belonged.

I spent a significant amount of time looking for "it" in a relationship with a man. I thought getting married was the only entry point to create a family of my own. Now in my late thirties, I couldn't ignore my screaming biological clock. Time was running out to make my "happily ever after" happen.

In the middle of accepting my life not turning out the way I planned, my mind opened up to greater possibilities. My grief drove me to look deeper into myself for answers. A few months earlier, writing in my journal, surrounded by tear-soaked snotty tissues, it struck me: "I don't want to have a baby – what I truly want is the chance to be a parent." And there were many ways to become a parent besides meeting a man, getting married and having a baby.

I had no idea what Lindsey would come to mean to me when we met. I didn't know becoming Lindsey's foster and then adoptive mother was going to be our story. And none of this was on my mind that January evening when I picked her up in that empty house.

Now, I looked across the table at Lindsey. She was working her way through something with lots of melted cheese, and a big plate of fries. This beautiful little soul was alone and hungry, and she had no place to go. I got it. There was no one else left to reach out to but me. The next move was mine.

It didn't matter that I didn't have the room, that my dog still pissed on my carpet, and that the house was a mess. My imperfect self, was enough to be who she needed this evening. I surrendered to the part I was called to play in Lindsey's life that night. I took the next indicated step.

"You don't want to stay in that empty house all by yourself, do you? I mean, it is scary isn't it?" I asked.

Lindsey lowered her voice. "No, I don't want to go back there."

"Well, I guess you'll come home with me tonight after we get Charlie some food. We can call social services again at my house. Is that OK?"

"Yes, OK, "Lindsey agreed.

Back home, clean and dirty clothes sprinkled my Berber carpeted suite. I smiled at how utterly unprepared I was for a guest, and how little it mattered.

When Lindsey came into my life, a friend said to me "You seemed so lost before you met Lindsey," and I was. Something was missing. I'd go from thinking about my past to daydreaming about the future, searching for clues to solve the puzzle.

With Lindsey in my space that night I became firmly planted in the present. It was as though I had been living suspended in mid-air. Finally, my feet could touch the ground. All I could focus on was, "What do I do now? What do I do next?"

We found an old air mattress for her to sleep on in the windowless closet we pretended was a bedroom. After we set up her bed, we went into my makeshift kitchen. I can see Lindsey standing in the kitchen, with her hands in the sink washing dishes. The way the light from the bathroom seeped out and backlit her tiny face made her look angelic.

Lindsey looked at me with such trust and relief and quietly said, "I never thought about God until I met you, Jane."

I put down the dish towel and for the first time that night, we stood together and started to cry.

I will always think of that messy kitchen as our birthing room. I didn't need to have a biological child to become a mother. This was our birth canal.

My life changed because I came to see *someone like me* could be a foster parent. I was exactly the right parent for Lindsey. She is the daughter meant for me. Together, Lindsey, me, Sam and Charlie became a family.

Look beneath the surface. An unconventional family is just *love* showing up in different clothes. There are many ways to create a family. And happily ever after can take many forms.

Jane's chapter is adapted from the memoir she and her daughter, Lindsey McNeill, are co-authoring entitled: "Daughters of the Divine."

About Jane

Jane is a professional coach dedicated to helping women wake up, speak up, show up strong and claim bigger dreams.

Jane knows first-hand that life doesn't always go as planned and our "happily ever after" sometimes gets derailed.

The good news is, if we tell the truth, we can create space for greater possibilities.

Getting back on track begins with painfully honest answers to two questions: "What is essential for me to be satisfied at this time in my work and life? Who do I need to become to achieve my definition of success?"

Countless times, Jane has witnessed the power of using this personal clarity as the foundation for work and life design. When coupled with the courage to take action and collaborate with others we need to succeed, transformation happens.

Jane specializes in coaching women who want to thrive at work they love, live the life they want and make collaboration with others work.

Contact Jane at www.janezakreski.com and see the full scope of Jane's work.

I AM a brilliant woman as I am loyal to my truth, and I dare to keep living it.

– Jane Zakreski

I AM Light

And We Rise

By Brandi Taylor

When I was a kid, I had the luxury of early childhood in a very abusive home. Yes, I did say luxury and before you flip past these pages and move on to the next chapter, give me a moment. With experiences come lessons and wisdom. These life-altering events give us the opportunity to learn. In my case, these lessons were tough but monumental. I had no idea that my first memory would alter my perception of fear, how I experienced it and just how debilitating fear would be for most of my life.

As adults, we experience life through the lenses established in childhood. Some healthy, some not. Mine were distorted through the abuse. When I was very young, there was a lot of yelling, anger and physical abuse in our home. My mother was terrified of my father who reigned with a fist. So, when I was three, my mother tried to leave. Standing at the door of the farmhouse, my sister and I in each arm, my mother attempted to leave. My father pulled a shotgun, pointed it at her head and said, "If you leave here with them I will kill you." This is my first memory. This traumatic event set the stage for so many hard lessons to come.

It took three more years of fists flying, yelling and soul-damaging abuse before the police took my father away. He was removed for another set of crimes, separate from the ones at home, that kept him from ever returning. He was sentenced to twenty-five years in prison. In the years that followed, my mother did the best she could with the knowledge and experiences she had. Though she loved us, she was still too broken herself to get involved in a healthy relationship. Self-worth and confidence did not develop in a healthy manner either. There was a lot of dysfunction trickling through in the form of discipline, acceptability and expectations.

The night my father was taken probably saved my life. If he had stayed, I don't know if I would have been strong enough to survive. Memories resurfaced one night when I was sixteen. For a sixteen-year-old memories and hormones are a lethal combination. That night I tried walking in front of a car. It was a half-ass attempt. A cry for help. In that car was an off-duty fireman. He took me to the hospital and had me admitted. I was assigned a therapist. In that only session, the therapist said, "You seem to have a pretty good grasp on this. You'll be fine." I left there with no understanding of the underlying destructive mechanisms I now carried or that I should have sought another therapist. The one thing I did know – I was stronger than suicide.

For the rest of my teens and early twenties I was an unknowing victim. I would create situations where I either tried to help fix someone or put myself into positions where people felt sorry for me. Each guy I dated – same problems only different faces. This pattern manifested so largely in a relationship when I was twenty-six there was no denying it was no longer them needing fixing.

Bob was a broken, damaged soul. He had family issues, a sad heart and in the end, a major drug addiction. We lived together for about a year and a half when I discovered his crack addiction. He would come into the house one morning angry and upset, pinned me to the bed, crying and threatened to kill himself and me. This was him coming down. It was then I called a distress centre. The volunteer had unwittingly given me a gift. Minutes in, while agreeing Bob needed to come in, he also suggested I come in, to learn how to cope of course. Reluctantly I booked the appointment. This first session proved pinnacle. In that hour we discussed Bob, which turned into my father, then my mother. I had issues. It was the first time someone got to the heart of real patterns.

Shortly after, I moved out. Started reading self-help books. While reading *Seat of the Soul* by Gary Zukov, I struggled with one chapter. Two weeks in and still not through it. This chapter was about responsibility - the role we play in every experience in our life. It was a call with a dear friend that opened me to this painful acknowledgement. She said to me, "You know, Brandi, we like to make ourselves the victims." This chapter was and still is the most profound lesson learned. I was responsible for what I let in and chose to accept in my life.

By choosing our actions instead of being reactive, we ultimately create more desirable outcomes. I began seeing how I had been a victim my whole life. That I created these situations, which in turn kept me in misery. I delved deep within. I felt depressed yet not. I felt like the world was on my shoulders. This work was dark, honest and heavy – the hardest thing I had ever done. By the time, I had finished the book, I realized my role. I had accepted and forgiven. Forgiving those in my life and myself. That was the hardest – forgiving myself. There was a lot of shame.

Shame belonging to others I had accepted as my own. Shame for the behaviours leading up to these realizations. And shame for giving away so much of myself to those unable to treat me with honour. But truly, how was someone to honour what I did not?

This time was the worst and best of my early life. It was here that I really began living. About a year later, I would meet a wonderful man that played a major role in my life for the next fifteen years and the father of my two boys. It is the demise of that relationship that has led me here today.

In abusive homes, there is subconscious acceptance of this behaviour. As an adult when I really started to explore this behaviour I learned some valuable things about my family and the cycle it had participated in. When I met my husband, I thought I had it all figured out. Turned out there were still patterns and tendencies to give over too much of myself to another. I needed to be stronger. I needed to stop allowing patterns of the past to haunt me. I just didn't really know they were still there leading the charge that was my life.

Fear had become such a strong subconscious driver I hadn't noticed it until it was too late. He had gone into a depression. I tried many tactics to get him to open up. He locked me out for the final five years. I was alone in a marriage. I was so afraid of hurting him more that I had allowed fear of speaking up, using my voice, sharing my opinion, to interfere with my marriage. He was hurting, so when I would speak up he would twist things around and put them on me. I just didn't stand up for myself, again. One night while out with girlfriends, a social worker friend brought everything to light. All the pieces I was unable to connect, she put together. She explained I didn't experience fear as fight or flight. I experienced it as life or death. With this revelation, everything made sense. This was why I always told myself to put on my big girl panties. Stop being a child. Act like an adult. I would have to talk myself into doing what needed doing.

It was my subconscious leaking through. It was so obvious once she said it. I was stuck in that moment at the door. Looking at the shotgun. Terrified. Trying to cope. I was frozen at the age of three.

It was after this, the real work started. I looked at different behaviours. Why was I staying when it was so broken? No love shared. My heart broke more each day but the worst of it was what I had given up in those years. I had given up pieces of myself so he could feel better. I had lessened myself, made myself smaller, so he didn't have to feel small or broken.

I was slowly snuffing out my own light. Slowly killing my spirit and all that was beautiful within me because I was too afraid to do what needed to be done.

We tried counselling. It didn't work.

As it turned out, a game would turn things around for me. It was my kedge. For someone that didn't play games, I stumbled into one. Chats were fun. People were interesting. Strategies were exciting. Battles were invigorating. We worked together.

Then came the chat.

A stand-alone chat for people playing this game. This room was wild. It was here that I began piecing myself back together.

Fragments came back. I started seeing the person I was. My true voice came back with all its might: funny, witty, desirable, depth of heart, empathy and joy. Simple joy was an element I had lost. Being desired – something I'd completely forgotten. Or as someone with a creative force that will not be denied. Or a person of strength and tenacity. I had forgotten the person I loved. The adventurous one. The fun one. The optimist. The creator.

I had forgotten me.

A few months later I told my husband I was done. This was the hardest step I have ever taken. I said I couldn't allow my light to go out. I would not be small anymore. I am a giant awakened. I will not go back to sleep. Ever.

Those words would be my guide. They changed everything about who I am today and who I will be tomorrow. I know now that holding back serves no one; not others, not me. I know now life is meant to be lived not compromised. No more settling. No more being someone I am not. I am a brilliant woman.

I realize I have been paralysed almost my whole life, settling for things other people wanted for me or expected of me. With eyes wide-open I see now I choose this life. That step, leaving my husband, was the first of many where I now take my fear with me and do it anyway.

Because I love myself more than any other. I need to do what is right for me. I choose not to make things fit in my life any longer. Instead I choose to find the things that fit. No more square pegs in round holes. Since that day in June I have separated, moved, started a new career and a new business and am about to launch a podcast called Fear It Goes. It's all about taking your fear with you and doing it anyway. Whether your challenges are small or large, know that the first step to changing them is the hardest.

I know now that all we are, all we want, all we need is all around us. It's time to take off the mask. The life we desire, the life we have always wanted has always been here. Ready for us to claim it. Live it. Be it.

Yet we are too comfortable.

We play too small, thinking this is all there is.

We are too afraid.

Afraid. Not always afraid of failure but more fearful of becoming our greatness within. Our biggest, brightest self, shining through for all the world to see. To judge. To deny. To envy. To hurt. Take the first step. Trust in what you want. Courage is not in the absence of fear. Courage is taking those steps and doing it anyway.

There are so many things I have learnt in this past six months. But one of the most profound is how to be who you are. How to take the wounds of the past and use them with purpose. These glorious, difficult experiences have made you the most beautiful unique person. Every single moment has brought you to who you are today. Without all the shame, the hurt, the debilitating fear, I never would have understood how to translate those lessons into helping others and guiding them on their journey to being whole. Change is a process with steps.

You can live the life you want. Yes, you can. Rise up.

Ask the universe this: "Why have I created the most spectacular or fulfilled life? Why am I so in love with my life? Why am I so lucky? Why am I so amazing?"

Bring about your greatness. Stand tall and don't ever give up on you. You can and will always be your biggest cheerleader. I'm cheering for you too. Be your Giant! Be your Greatness! Everything else falls into place.

And we rise...

About Brandi

Brandi Taylor is a creator, a busy mom of two crazy boys (and she wouldn't have it any other way), a hockey mom and sometimes, well, a taxi. She has lifted others up and flushed lives down toilets, authoring fiction. Coming from a filmmaker background she assumed the transition from screenplay to manuscript would be easy. After a few years of night school and a yearlong novel writing/critiquing course, laying down parts of a four-book series, she figured it out and wrote her first stand-alone suspense thriller - Missing Piece - currently editing. Her latest work - And We Rise - is a nonfiction piece.

By day, she is a business development manager but by night, a unicorn trying to change the world. She is busy launching a podcast called, *Fear It Goes,* which is all about taking your fears with you and doing it anyway. Her first episode is, "Pooping My Pants But Doing It Anyway." Because that's just the way it is, and she says it's time we got out of this zone we call comfort and achieve what we really want – *a life on fire.*

I AM a brilliant woman for courageous action taken to help others rise up with me.

– Brandi Taylor

I AM Perseverance

Remembering the Woman I AM

By Tessa Labbe

If you are a mom you may have had those days where you think, "Look how fat I've gotten, I'm so tired, I'm feeling so depressed, I've been in my pajamas the last three days, what have I done today!? I've been puked on, I've changed dirty diapers and I have dealt with a screaming infant while our toddler destroyed our house."

Feeling your baby inside your womb turning and kicking is such a gift. Unless you have experienced it, you cannot truly imagine how grand it is. And I want you to know I love my kids. So you think that would make me feel good, being a mom!?

"How come I feel so lost, so depressed and I don't even know who I am anymore? Did I ever know? What I would give to see just a hint of who I am as a woman not just Mom."

Does any of this sound familiar?

Everyone is so eager to tell us how amazing motherhood is yet they forget to state how physically, mentally and emotionally exhausting it is. Our stomach stretches far out past our feet, bellies become road maps of stretch marks, our body swells as we retain water, we carry a human who is growing inside for nine months so our instinct to be more safe is heightened, our hormones go wacky like they are having a college dance party, our hips spread like butter on toast and let's never speak of how stretched our vagina is.

How come no one discusses the aftermath all this has on us as women? It's the:

Woman who suffers with post pardon depression.

Woman who receives lack of empathy from her spouse

Woman who cannot get their baby to stop crying.

Woman who tore so bad during labor she cannot walk for the first week after her baby's birth.

Woman who feels pressure from society to breastfeed yet she struggles every day having her baby latch.

Becoming a mother is truly a gift from God and at the same time many women lose who they are. Why should we as women feel pressured to give our kids and husbands everything? Why do we forget about our true identity?

Being a mom means you were up all night baking your kid's class gluten free cupcakes (that taste like cardboard) with no dairy for his/her birthday; you must meet all the dietary needs of the kids and they're not thankful for the gesture. You are up all night with restless kids, yet up at the crack of dawn primping yourself to look flawless so others think you have this mom thing down to an art.

I was once told, "It's all smoke and mirrors my friend." Why? Why must we place this much stress onto ourselves and others just to be fake? Instead, let's admit to the challenges of motherhood, find out who we are again aside from our kids and husbands. Why don't we stand together as *empowered* and *brilliant* women living the life we all deserve?

Hi, I'm Tessa. God placed me on this Earth as a daughter, sister, granddaughter and niece. Soon I became an athlete, a student and a friend. I was Tessa. I loved to laugh, play dolls, ride my bike and travel for judo tournaments.

As years went on, I became a girlfriend who then became a wife at twenty-two years old. And somewhere I lost myself. I lost the *Woman Tessa*. I was now, Wife Tessa and Collin. We enjoyed snowboarding, camping, watching movies and hanging out with friends.

Twenty-three came and everything changed. I was now Mom Tessa and *Woman Tessa* seemed to be placed on the shelf in the closet while this exhausted yet happy mother came alive. After my daughter was born, my sister-in-law told me that she was eager to watch me get fat. Well, that comment unleashed *Woman Tessa* and I was on fire. I joined a boot camp and got into the best shape I had been in a long time.

Seventeen months later, we were blessed with baby number two. Sadly, *Woman Tessa* was placed on the shelf once again and there she stayed for quite awhile. Being a mom was my new reality. Mom Tessa was in charge; she was tired, frustrated and excited all at the same time. Mom Tessa loves being a mom, but let's face it, it is a hard, tiring, thankless, dirty and very repetitive job. This mama hated cleaning house daily while what seemed to be living in her pajamas. I wanted *Woman Tessa* back in the picture. I wanted the best of both worlds, yet it felt like too much to ask for. I wanted friends, family, strangers and me to know *Woman Tessa*; and after all these years, who was I? I was no longer a judoka, no longer a rugby player, and no longer an employee... who was I? I was determined to find out.

Fitness Kickboxing Instructor you say... Oh yes please! This had *Woman Tessa* written ALL over it. Went for a weekend hands-on course, I felt so alive, studied at home during my kids' naptime. (Oh, who was I kidding!) My kids cut that precious time out as soon as they could. My studying had to be during the evenings and now I was a certified Fitness Kickboxing Instructor.

I searched out a spot to rent, advertised in the papers (social media was not like it is now) and prayed to God clients would come. How did I do this? I was never a mom who let my babies consume every day of my life. If I wanted to go shopping with a girlfriend, my kids came. If I needed to talk to a business about rentals, my kids came. I loved being the creator of something different in town that women seemed to gravitate to; however, my business sense was zero. Renting space for classes was becoming more and more difficult, I had to chase clients to pay their fees and my hubby worked up north so I was juggling two toddlers, my business, finding childcare and commuting. My plate was full.

My evening classes were rushed so I could come home and have my kids in bed at a proper time and my morning classes were even more rushed from being exhausted from a sleepless night, packing up my kids to be early enough to set up for class and be prepared for my clients. I eventually certified two women so they could help me instruct.

Two years later, pregnant with baby number three, a lot of money invested into my business, I decided to sell my equipment and say good-bye to my business. I felt the world was against me. I felt like a huge failure. How was *Business Woman Tessa* to be part of me when she couldn't even juggle her business and home life? I had met amazing women, women who looked up to me as they saw their body change and never thought it was possible. So, why couldn't I make this business life and mom life work together?

After more sleepless nights, dirty diapers, camping trips, birthdays and now school days, I needed to connect with my inner *Woman Tessa* once more. I hired a live out nanny so I could work full time. I LOVED it! I had a job that challenged my brain rather than worrying what toilet needed scrubbing. I had my own workspace and I felt I could breathe again. When I came home from work, my kids were excited to see me and I was excited to see them. And since the nanny cooked dinner, I could treasure our time together as a family more every night. At work, I was *Business Woman Tessa,* enjoying adult conversations and making new friends and then at home in the evening, a mom who enjoyed her snuggles, bath time, and reading stories before bed. Life was falling into place perfectly.

The kids were often sick with colds or the flu, which meant I had to miss work to take them to doctor appointments. Or I would be sitting at work talking and texting my nanny giving doctors' updates and attempting to understand what he was diagnosing them with. We ran into major potty training setbacks with our youngest, which led to weekly pediatrician appointments. Life became this circus and my juggling everything became the main event.

Eventually, I started feeling jealous of my nanny for she was raising *my* kids and making the memories I should have been making. I mean I had kids because as far as I could remember I wanted to raise a family, laugh, snuggle, make the tears disappear and teach them strength, hope and love but at the same time, I NEEDED *Woman Tessa* to be part of my life too. So, day by day the juggling act continued. To top it off, I woke one day to such pain in my feet I could barely walk. Doctor appointment after appointment, months passing by, I was finally diagnosed with Rheumatoid Arthritis. At twenty-eight years old, I was falling apart at the seams and couldn't seem to get stitched back up.

Nanny soon moved on and kids entered daycare. Our mornings were now full of juggling four people getting fed and dressed, dropping them off by a certain time so I could get to work on time and paying outrageous amount in daycare fees.

Was my job worth the mental and physical exhaustion?

After two years, another job over. Home to heal myself and raise my babies.

We enjoyed a two-week trip to Florida and a Disney Cruise, I attended my son's Kindergarten Grad (the happy tears that fell… sigh), we enjoyed summer days at our lake lot and I could have coffee dates with my friends.

Life moves fast and ours was non-stop.

Three kids now in school, this mom felt a freedom she had never felt. Two and a half hours every morning to myself! Then I wondered, how did we get to this point in our lives so fast? I was determined to embrace my time as mom with my kids. Fires in the yard, kid mud fights, volunteering for field trips, enjoying my mommy/daughter afternoons, and went skydiving with my mom.

Over the years, I searched for a business that would ignite a fire in me and after a few failed attempts; I finally found something I was passionate about. I received my wedding planning certification and launched my business around my schedule and around my kids. I was no longer going to live our lives around work. Work would now be based around my family.

As my kids grew older, I was able to be a great mom and also enjoy the woman within. Even though, I love being a mom, I also felt God placed me on this earth for more.

I am now embracing and loving both *Mom Tessa* and *Woman Tessa*. And look, I am an author in a book! How did that even happen? I never in a million years imagined this would be me. My journey of integrating my true identity as a woman has been a long emotional road. After twelve years, I am still working on balance and I will never give up; no woman ever should. We are women; strong, beautiful, intelligent and that's how we should see ourselves. I am proud to be a mom, and finally having the chance to experience *Tessa* coming alive more and more every day is a true blessing. The path to finding the priceless gems in our souls is not easy; nothing in life that is worth your time and energy comes easy. We just need to learn to accept that and make the greatness happen through the good and the bad.

Three ways to embrace your brilliance and find the "Woman" in you are:

One: Read, *The Emotional Edge* by Crystal Andrus Morissette. Find where you are failing right now in your life: Mother energy, Daughter energy or Woman energy. From there you can take day by day learning to embrace all parts of you and have all those parts work together.

Two: Surround yourself with like-minded, empowered, positive women. You will become who you surround yourself with. Will everyday be a keg party full of laughs and old times... NO, but the women who can see past the drag and build each other up are the ones you will want to be around. Positive = Positive, Negative = Negative.

Three: Take life day by day. Don't get caught up worrying about what will happen two weeks from now or even one month from now. Every little step forward will eventually lead you to the big, major picture you want for your life and soul.

About Tessa

Tessa Labbe is an ambitious woman who strives daily to be the best version of herself.

As a successful distributer for a premium skin care company, Tessa connects with women, coaching them as they grow their ideal life, business and self-confidence.

Studying to become an Empowerment Coach with S.W.A.T. Institute, she is devoted to helping women across the globe achieve their inner woman, peace and endless possibilities.

As a mother of three, Tessa believes teaching her kids to be loving, strong, genuine, motivating, consistent and true to who they are will help them to overcome life's boundaries, allowing them to soar to great heights.

Tessa volunteers with the Junior League of Edmonton to connect with more amazing women within her community and feels it is a way to give back to her community.

Tessa can be contacted at tlabbe.myrandf.com/ca/

I AM a brilliant woman placed on earth to thrive and help other women thrive.

– Tessa Labbe

I AM Daring

Daring to…

By Joanne Neweduk

I sat on the bottom step of my stairwell with my face buried in my hands, fighting back tears. I felt absolutely wretched. I had thrown my back out, was in tremendous pain and had trouble moving. More painful, however, was that I understood my marriage was crumbling. In that moment, I needed support and caring, but instead, we were embroiled in a ridiculous argument that involved: bitterness, contempt, disappointment and hurt. It was a stressful time in my life. I was a full-time mom with three young, busy children, an aging, ill parent, a workaholic husband and this sick fear that all I held dear was going to shatter. I loved our life, but I was stressed by our roller coaster relationship. I felt responsible for everyone else's health and happiness and had lost sight of my own. I love being in service and helping others, but at that time, there was little reciprocity, so I was no longer acting from a stance of power, but instead, one of duty with the sense

95

that I had little choice. My life mostly revolved around helping others fulfill their dreams, yet no one asked me what my dreams were, least of all myself. Perhaps it was because I had forgotten how to dream.

It would be several years before the reality of divorce came to pass. About ten years ago, that major life event rocked me to my core and sent all I held dear into question. At the time, it felt as if all my worst fears had come true, as I so strongly believed we could make it. I now see it is a blessing and the catalyst that helped me become a brilliant woman and embrace joy and happiness as my most comfortable state of being. Gratitude, celebration and generosity (to myself and others) are now at the core of my daily practices.

Back then, I was not accustomed to asking for help and being supported. I was the strong one who helped everyone else, so this period of time was humbling, and a road of many lessons. I cried on my friends' shoulders, I vowed that I would do everything possible to ensure that this breakup would affect my children as little as possible, and most importantly, I took chances and opportunities to grow and I dared to dream.

I deepened friendships and my spirituality; I attended workshops on personal development; I travelled to the other side of our planet; I opened up to a new deeper love; and I generally embraced amazing opportunities that have led me to where I am now. I learned to wash off that mud of life that was weighing me down and hiding my joy and ability to dream. I released fear and overwhelm; sadness and disappointment, hurt and embarrassment. I released the belief I needed to be everything for everyone. I released the sense of failing. I learned that being super mom means relaxing into who I am at my core. Being vulnerable and trusting that I would be supported is the magic that transformed my life. I learned to embrace the innate, inner strength and brilliant light that I possess, and allowed it to shine more and more and, yes, I felt vulnerable at times.

Dare to be Supported

One story I recall occurred when I was invited to attend a sweat lodge. I desperately wanted to be part of this incredible opportunity, but feared that I might not be able to handle the experience due to a health issue. I feared that I might spoil the event for the others. My old self simply would have declined and missed out on the opportunity. Instead, I plucked up my courage to speak to the organizer and shared my fears. She looked at me with compassion and, in a matter-of-fact way, touched my arm and declared, "Well, if you don't feel well, we'll simply take care of you. You'll sit by me just in case." Emotion bubbled up inside of me. I knew I would be safe and, indeed, that evening was one of the most unique and incredible experiences I have ever had. That night, I had the humbling opportunity to receive care and love and it transformed me. A layer of mud was washed away.

Today, I am so very grateful for experiences like this because I often work with people who struggle with self-care or accepting support. This has fostered my ability to create a safe space for the strong to be vulnerable. This ability has come in handy in all my roles, both personally and professionally.

Dare to Adventure

I mentioned that I started to open up to stepping past fear and saying yes to opportunities. One such opportunity was travelling to Nepal and India with the humanitarian organization Medical Mercy Canada. This had been a longstanding dream of mine. I had been on their board of directors for many years, organizing fundraising events, and longed to travel overseas with one of the volunteer teams.

A few years ago a girlfriend declared she wanted to do a humanitarian trip. The die was cast for an amazing adventure on the other side of the world with two wonderful friends and an incredible charity. Many of the people we met in Nepal were desperately poor by our standards, yet I witnessed them in deep gratitude for the care they received. They were generous with what little they had, and we all had fun celebrating together with music and dancing. My friends and I also traveled in India to see places that have stood for millennia. It was a magical, life-changing trip and a dream come true.

For several years, I was without a partner, with only the occasional flirtation. I knew it was important to be happy on my own before I could be happy with someone new. After a time, I felt ready to invite romantic love back into my life. The prospect of dating again in my late forties was a bit daunting and I really wasn't certain how to go about this project.

I chose to focus on, and manifest, a relationship based on mutual love, respect and support while filled with fun and adventure. A friend strongly encouraged me to go on eHarmony for a few months, so I did. I had email conversations with a couple of nice gentleman and even met one for coffee, but nothing materialized. Nothing captured me. In the last week that I planned to be on the site, I noticed a man whose eyes smiled with genuine warmth and caring. I plucked up courage to say hello, which started a wonderful exchange of email letters for a couple of weeks. This was followed by a meeting for coffee, which turned into a date that lasted for hours. A few days later, we went on a dinner date that left me day-dreaming on the drive home to the point that I missed my turn and needed to take the long way around. My highest compliment for a man is that he is strong enough to be gentle, confident without arrogance and is protective without being possessive. This is what I had found. There were things about myself I wasn't sure I liked anymore because these had been aspects of me that were most criticized. Yet these were the things he would declare he loved most about me. Layers of emotional mud washed away as we both opened ourselves up for new love.

When I was first separated, one of my friends had compassionately listened to my woes. She herself was in a beautiful relationship which I longed to emulate. She looked at me sweetly, and softly said, "You deserve to be cherished." That struck me intensely. At the time, that was hard to even imagine, but I held on to that nugget.

For over six years now, Ron and I have been co-creating a relationship that we both cherish. Every day we feel a deep sense of gratitude for how fortunate we are to be experiencing this next chapter in our lives. It is beautiful to make dreams together while we each also have our own dreams that we both support and encourage. Combined, we have five adult children, in various stages of being launched or at university. We love watching them develop into incredible, unique individuals. Our hearts are warmed to see them get along and have fun together.

Dare to be YOU... Without the Mud

I like to relate my healing story in an analogy. It helps me gain perspective, especially when I get tripped up in life. I use this in speeches, coaching and meditations to support others.

When I was in the throes of unhappy life circumstances, it felt like I was sitting in a deep mucky pit. I couldn't see the light above me nor believe that life could be better. I was so covered with the mud of life's hurts that I had lost perspective on what was mine to own and what was not. I knew if I stayed there or continued to blame others for me being there, I could slip into on-going victimhood. Sometimes people climb out of the pit with sheer grit and anger but never take the time to acknowledge or process the pain they have been through. When that happens, the mud stays on and our inner light is hidden, even when we don't realize it. Until I started to get that emotional mud washed off, I didn't even know it was there.

Often, people just go walking through life and don't even realize they feel so awful because they are carrying that emotional muck. They are resigned to thinking that's just how they are and there is no hope. From my experiences, I know that there is always hope and a way to heal. There is always something or someone able to help us climb out of that pit and wash off.

When I chose to get healthier, with support, I climbed out of the mud, rinsed off and initially felt amazing. The difference between where I had been and where I stood was incredible. I trotted off feeling great, but with time and increased awareness I recognized I still had a layer of dried mud. (It loves to hide in unseen spaces, like sand after a day at the beach.) It was also very easy to trip up again and land back in muck. I realized I was due for some further exploration of what I wanted in life and an increase in valuable self-care skills. This phase is like taking a metaphorical hot, soapy shower to scrub away the residual film for a deeper healing.

I felt healthier and happier. I knew I might still trip and land in the mud; it happens, of course, but by now I could get out faster and I knew how to shower off the mud right away. I knew that mud did not belong on me.

The next phase is what I love best, as it is like slathering on luscious creams and oils to prevent the mud from sticking in the first place. This is the phase I choose to function within. It is one of deepened self-awareness, strengthened spiritual connection and increased self-care practices so that I know how to avoid the muck... most of the time. But when I can't, it simply doesn't stick like it used to.

Using this analogy has helped me assess where I am on my journey at any given time. When I have stress, or a recurrent issue, it means I need to look at my beliefs around that issue, heal an old hurt, or focus my self-care practices of daily gratitude, generosity and celebration. Through this process, I have transformed my life and relationships.

Over the years, I have been willing to say yes to incredible opportunities. Bit by bit, I have washed off the mud, dared to dream and now truly delight in supporting others to do the same.

Three life changing nuggets that have empowered me to be the brilliant woman I am today:

One: Graciously accept support

One of the greatest lessons I have ever learned is to graciously receive. Giving and receiving are two sides of the same coin and it is not possible to have one without the other. When we are not willing to embrace both, we stagnate the flow of love energy within our relationships. Through my own experiences, I now realize that refusing to accept support is actually quite selfish. It deprives people of the opportunity to give. Graciously receiving is humbling and a beautiful gift we offer to ourselves and others.

Two: Be open to love and adventure

Being open to something new, even when it scares you, is an adventure. Love being the greatest of these. Whether your adventure is traveling around the world, returning to school or co-creating a new loving relationship, stepping through that fear is vital to creating a zest for life.

Three: You are not the mud

Life gets muddy at times. We get splashed, sometimes fully covered... It's our responsibility to remember to wash off that mud regularly. To remember we are NOT the mud. We get to choose whether we leave it on, allowing it to weigh us down, or use it to scrub ourselves fresh, making us healthier and more radiant, ready to face a new day as a Brilliant Woman and daring to dream.

About Joanne

Joanne Neweduk is a nurse, author, coach, speaker and facilitator. She is the founder of Brilliant Light Wellness where she blends her skills of wellness coaching, light therapy, Sound Wellness, and Belief Re-patterning to shed light on health and happiness, believing there is always hope for both. Joanne also runs Fabulous@50 Calgary, which empowers, educates and celebrates women in midlife.

Joanne's favourite self-care acts are explorations on gratitude, generosity and celebration. She contributes to the Be Fabulous e-magazine and is featured in the award winning books:

Women Who Rock 2

Frock Off: Living Undisguised

Fabulous@50 The Re-Experience

Joanne has a decades-long involvement with volunteerism, event planning and is currently the past president of a humanitarian charity, Medical Mercy Canada. She is enthusiastic with every endeavour she takes on and derives great joy from collaborating with others and seeing wonderful things transpire.

Above all, Joanne's greatest joy is her family.

I AM a brilliant woman who dares to dream.

– Joanne Neweduk

I AM Honour

I Choose Me

By Trina Rowsell

While driving through the Rocky Mountains with my mother on a bright summer afternoon several years ago, I made the comment, "Mother, you've never really liked me."

To which she responded, "Trina, I've always loved you." "Yes, Mother," I said, "but you've never liked me."

My mother once again responded, "I've always loved you."

"Yes, mother," I said again, "I know you love me as a daughter, but you've never really liked me."

She paused for a moment, then said, "You're right. From the time you could dress yourself, your clothes always had to be perfect and you had to dance for everyone. The way you enunciate your words and your need to carry yourself perfectly. You never stopped talking. This drove me nuts."

Even though my mother accepts me for who I am today, these words clarified how I felt most of my life – always thinking I would never be enough.

As a young girl, I enjoyed clothes and wore a lot of dresses. I loved to dance and performed for my parents' friends and anyone who was willing to pay attention. My parents even put me in tap and jazz–which I loved, as I got to perform on stage for large audiences. The freedom of dancing filled me with so much joy.

One day, while practicing my dance routine with my best friends, they told me I was fat and that I could not dance nor was I as good as them. I was confused. At eight years old, my world crumbled. I didn't understand why my best friends said these mean things to me. I loved dancing and believed I was quite good. I came home that night and for several nights afterwards I prayed to God to make me skinny, and I became sadder about my body image each morning when I woke looking the same.

Over time, I created my own reality and became the caregiver for everyone as a way to bring a level of peace and normalcy to my world. My father drank, a lot. My parents' anger and abuse towards each other was at times unbearably scary and shut me down. Friends rarely came to my house, nor did we have much money. I never felt like I belonged as my family was different from my friends' families, and, at times, I wanted their lives. At a young age, I was sexually abused and felt pushed aside by everyone I cared for. I felt judged and unworthy. I became bulimic, and, in turn was pushing most everyone away that tried to get close to me. This became a pattern that ran deep.

My childhood shaped me. The time between flourishing as a child to early adulthood was not easy. Although I experienced many defining moments in the earlier part of my life, three clearly stand out. One could say these were soul-crushing moments. The first was the one I mentioned above, when my friends called me fat and that I was not good enough to dance. The second was sexual abuse from men close to me in my life with most of these memories blocked out for some time. The third experience was when I was rejected by my first serious boyfriend as I gained a lot of weight and lost myself during our relationship. This final experience was the proverbial nail in my coffin as I fully shut down from accepting love in my life, from myself or anyone. This experience brought up a lot of past trauma around rejection from people I cared about and further spun me into self-hatred and destructive behaviours that I allowed to define me.

How did I cope? Well, after years of partying to hide my sorrows and the perceived freedom, I dug deep into who I really was and who I desired to become. However, before I discovered my brilliant self, I became the master of the phrase, *fake it until you make it,* as I did not want anyone to know the deep sorrow within. As an adult, I used similar patterns from my childhood where I wore a mask to pretend everything was okay in order to escape my pain and the shifting landscape of my life. I wore perfection perfectly, or so I thought! I never felt good enough and sought validation from anyone who was willing to give it. And when I received a lot of attention I would create even more drama. One could say I was addicted to the cycle.

Over time, I developed patterns that on the surface kept me safe and what I didn't realize was that, internally, the light of my soul was being buried. I wanted men to love and validate me, yet I would walk away before they got close enough. Most of my friendships were shifting as I pushed my friends away, too. I was starting to feel alone and isolated.

The intellect in me knew what I was doing with all my relationships. I would make small shifts to return to feeling whole, and then I would repeat destructive patterns, typically around men and money. You see, I have the capacity to make what some would say is a lot of money. I had less capacity to respect my brilliance and let this grow; I spent all of the money I earned until I had nothing left. I was well put together, which was my way of showing the world that I was excelling in life even though I had a mountain of debt that I ignored. I'd pay the debt and deal with collectors, then accumulate more. Rinse and repeat.

I dated kind and brilliant men, but always found something wrong. What I learned years later was that I never felt like I was enough nor did I have enough self-love or self-respect to choose me.

A few years ago, I moved to Vancouver, British Columbia after playing in the backcountry and feeling a sense of connection to the land. After several months being in that beautiful city, I could not find work even though I'm a highly skilled, intelligent woman. I was feeling stuck and drowning in more debt. On a typical rainy winter day in Vancouver, I was making lunch and trying to cut into a frozen bun. The next thing I knew, I was uncontrollably sobbing on the floor for what seemed like hours. I felt out of control and did not understand what was happening. These moments on the kitchen floor made me take a long hard look at the life I was choosing. I felt like I hit rock bottom.

Even though I had over fifteen years of training ranging from energetics and spirituality to leadership and technical areas, I was not able to shift my patterns as I continually felt hopeless and unworthy.

I called one of my greatest mentors to dig deeper into what was holding me back and controlling my life. I looked at what was keeping me in my perceived safe place and slowly began shifting my patterns of hurting most everyone around me by trying to control situations. I used money to validate myself or as a power play tool and even used my innate kindness to manipulate people to get what I desired.

I made a conscious choice to create the personal space to integrate and use tools to guide me in becoming the amazing human I knew I was, and desperately desired to be. I found peace near the water and daily took time to sit quietly. I retrained with my Shamanic community so that I could take my learning even deeper. I became a coach and leadership facilitator, which reminded me of my super powers! I even became a holistic nutritional consultant to learn more about the human body. I had the courage to look deeply at who I was and how I was not showing up in my life. I had the courage to take steps, move forward and further make changes so that I fully showed up in my life.

What I know to be true today is that those in my life did the best they could with the tools they had at the time. I've become an inspiring woman that has stepped into my power and created a life that is full of expression, joy and love for the world that I live in. I choose me so that I'm able to stand exactly as I am, balanced and in my power while modeling the behavior I want to see in the world. Every day, I get the opportunity to engage with other amazing humans from senior executives to a budding teenager to help them also see their brilliance. I weave in aspects of science and spirituality as they complement all aspects of my life. Communication and engaging other cool humans has become one of my super powers! This life is far too juicy to let the past keep me from living the extraordinary life I want.

My desire for you is to lead an even more brilliant life and to support this, I will share a few final thoughts. I have one caveat: whatever you do, please have fun!

One: Get to know yourself

Get to know yourself. This is something I feel strongly about as I used to let others define me and looked outside of myself for validation. I mean really know yourself and be comfortable enough to take a loving look at yourself in the mirror. Please, for the love of your soul, find a coach you trust. This experience is priceless. Find a coach that sees you and knows how to gently push you to see your patterns and finds many ways to help you shift. A great coach will make you squirm in your seat as you get uncomfortable. Awareness is key. Once I knew about my behaviour and patterns, I could not look back. Awareness allowed me to consciously make a choice to do something differently. We always have a choice.

Two: Find ways to light your soul

Life can be hard. Find ways to honour and inspire yourself that make your soul glow so that you can sail in the turbulent waters and still look in the mirror and tell yourself how beautiful you are. By the way, did I tell you that self-love is key to your freedom? When is the last time you looked in the mirror and told yourself how beautiful you are? Told yourself how proud you are of what you achieved today? When is the last time you took yourself on a date because you deserve only the best in your life?

Discover what lights your soul, whether physical activities, sports, serving your community, music, dance, hobbies, introspection, self-care. Discover what lights you up and do this!

Three: Choose yourself every day

Fall madly in love with yourself. Choose to live a life full of heart-centered experiences. Consciously choose an extraordinary life full of ease, play, joy! Perfection does not exist. Humans change every day as we ebb and flow through life and discover more about ourselves. You will change, as will those around you – it's OK. This life is full of beauty and experiences that mould us. Nobody gets to define who you are, you have all the power within yourself to honour your brilliance.

Repeat to yourself, "I consciously choose myself every day and I am grateful to have inspiring, loving relationships with those I also choose in my life."

Four: Remember, you are more than enough

Deep self-love takes a tremendous amount of patience as you intimately get to know yourself, and as you learn a new way of being. Those around you will also need patience as you begin to shift and become the brilliant human you've always been! There is no better way in this life to see your brilliance than to play in the process, find other cool humans that inspire you, discover what you love doing and then do it! Remember: lighten up a little and have fun! Be courageous and create loving boundaries for yourself that honour what you need. You deserve greatness in all levels of your life.

I need you to take one courageous step at a time. Be patient with yourself. Love yourself up. And please remember to look in the mirror to remind yourself of the bright shining star you are. Every day until this becomes habit. Remind yourself of your brilliance!

About Trina

Trina Rowsell believes the power of our soul runs deep and that everyone can create their desired freedom by looking at the emotional, mental, physical and spiritual aspects of our lives. Trina allowed the world to define who she was as she hid the trauma from years of abuse, depression, failed relationships and continually sought the idealistic view of the world, perfection.

Trina deeply believes in the freedom of knowing your authentic self and taking one courageous step to dig deep. To allow your greatest potential to unfold and create the life you desire – whether family, personal health, wealth or business goals, anything is possible. She also believes ultimate happiness is becoming unapologetic through the expression of who you truly are, allowing your soul to shine and never dim again.

As a trained Shaman, Authentic Leadership Facilitator, Holistic Nutritional Consultant, Inspirational Coach and Change Leader, Trina has over twenty years of corporate and community experience that continues to lead her to the path of freedom. Her approach and skills are flexible, practical and targeted to empower you to choose the path you always desired in this life!

You can connect with Trina at www.trinarowsell.com

I AM a brilliant woman because I choose not to be defined by my fears.

–Trina Rowsell

I AM Courage

Behind the Mask

By *Florence Shustack*

Can you imagine losing the one thing, that one trait or defining characteristic that you always believed you would possess? We all experience loss in its many shapes, shades, forms and sizes over our lifetime. We all learn at some point to deal with the loss of a friend, a pet, a family member, a place of residence, health, relationships, income and all scenarios we have been through individually or collectively or have experienced directly or indirectly. Somehow, we manage to cope with the grief, the aftermath and adjust to a *new* normal. But what would you do if you were stripped of that one thing that gave you the strength to continue? And what if that one thing defined your identity and your persona and without it you were reduced to an "empty shell," a lifeless form without passion, purpose or direction and a shadow of your former self? Can you imagine?

Well, it happened to me. My reason for living, belonging and what had brought a sense of purpose and great joy was gone.

A few years ago, my identity as a singer had come to an end and life had given me no warning. I had been known as a great singer for several decades. My voice began to spasm, glitch, falter and seize up during rehearsals and performances, and at times I felt as though I was choking. I knew something was seriously wrong, beyond the usual worrisome or troublesome symptoms of laryngitis or bronchitis. This sequence of events happened over a short period of time. Why it happened remains to be determined and I may never have an absolute answer. I felt betrayed by life.

Perhaps I simply had not paid attention to the signs, because my way was to push through everything, my way was survival, my way was to overcome everything, no matter what. In this defining instance or series of events, the "mask" was gone. There was nowhere to escape. My persona and career were flat-lined. It had taken me decades to achieve what I believed I was, a "singing star." I was requested and sought after, and on the precipice of a recording and touring career. My voice was dissolving and disintegrating; that "voice" for which I had become known and even famous to a certain extent. Even when I spoke, I began to sound like a cross between Pumbaa from *The Lion King* and Gollum from *The Hobbit*. The only way I could cope was to joke about it.

I realized I had spent my entire life grappling with identity as the daughter and first-born of a Holocaust survivor, who herself had endured unspeakable horrors and lost most of her family in the war.

Growing up, I was awkward, chunky, clumsy, shy, crying in school bathrooms because I was so sensitive to being made fun of or feeling embarrassed, hiding behind 'veils' and playing dress up in my mother's linens, or engrossed in books, particularly biographies. Two events in Grade 4 shaped what was to follow. In one instance, I was not chosen to be part of the school choir. But I went to practices and rehearsals anyway. In the second, I could not get a costume to fit me, because I had not realized there was a zipper. The event resulted in the entirety of the classroom laughing and mocking me, and needless to say, that sent me back to the bathroom in tears.

I worked hard and took on more responsibility. I did this for my mother and all I really wanted was to see her smile and for her to be proud of me. Yet no matter what I did, I was never the best.

To remove the mask would expose the hurt, the disappointment and feeling like a failure and a fraud. I think this must have been the time I developed and perfected the *Flo-smile,* which I was able to call upon at a moment's notice whenever it was necessary.

I groomed myself into the perfect young adult. I chose occupational therapy instead of medicine. I graduated number two with distinction. (Faculty of Medicine/Physical and Occupational Therapy.) My mother was prouder than proud.

From that moment on, I knew I had to be number one at something. Every position I took on, from being the first psychiatric occupational therapist at the Foothills Hospital and assuming a multitude of volunteer chairman roles for a number of organizations through the Jewish Community Centre, to taking dance classes, to doing my Western Board Conservatory in voice later in life, I wore my mantle proudly, and relentlessly and vigorously forged ahead.

When my mother lay in intensive care at the hospital on a Mother's Day, drawing her last breaths, I was able to comfort her, singing her favourite Jewish tunes. My singing voice was a given. Not long thereafter, while still working as an OT and raising two young children, I became known as "Dyna flow." I fronted orchestras and was known in the community as "The Simcha Singer," jokingly as "The Hora Queen," and more lovingly as "Florence, The Nightingale of Song."

There was no song I could not sing and it seemed I was unstoppable, indestructible, even when breast cancer found its way to me about ten years ago. I kept going. I did what I had to do. I stared in the mirror and saw my late mother's face and knew that if she had endured everything she went through to have me, I would not give up or give in.

Fast forward to the year of definition. On my birthday, June 8th, I pulled the plug on my career in the middle of a gig. I was struggling to continue and I knew I could not. I turned around to my band mates and asked them to please take over for the remainder of the evening. I was exhausted, frustrated and finished. I ached, had no voice to speak of–much less the voice of a nightingale–and all I could do was cry behind closed doors.

What followed was a year of tests and treatments. I tried everything to find answers, everything that offered any glimmer of hope, and, ultimately, there were no explanations. I became increasingly ill and had difficulty breathing and walking and I was unable to work. I was tired of struggling this time. Every ounce of me had wanted to get better and find a "cure," but this time, all seemed hopeless. I felt powerless. The mask had been ripped off, shredded and thrown away while any vestige of my former persona was soon to be discarded as I felt no longer wanted or useful.

I remember lying in bed one day and hearing only the startling sound of silence. No phone calls, only a few concerned friends (eventually fewer and fewer as my presence became more obscure). My young adult children were busy with their own lives and there was no relationship upon which to lean. Did anyone notice that I was not around? I felt like a nobody. What could I do with no voice? Even my speaking voice would dissolve while trying to communicate with others.

I could find no reason to live. I could go on to write paragraphs of feeling like a stranger in a strange land, no longer part of the musical community in which I had invested so much. I even felt invisible in the Jewish community where I held events, celebrations, music shows and volunteered. It was the most painful feeling.

So what brought me back to wanting to remain in the land of the living and not the walking dead?

I was led to my "calling" because I held on long enough to hear the words from a certain business coach. Have faith. After hearing my story, he told me, "Flo, you are like a Super-Olympic vocal coach with everything you know, have been through, have accomplished and are." At first, I did not believe I deserved to be called that. But I listened and allowed my heart to follow. I became a woman with a mission and my "why" became crystal clear. I had already been a voice coach, teaching out of my studio for a decade prior, but when the bottom fell out and I was no longer able to get back on that professional stage and perform, my vision led me to evolve and elevate my studio into something far greater with fervor, determination and for the greater good of others.

I would say I found my chutzpah (courage) but it was uncomfortable for me with a handicapped voice. I forced myself out the door to business meetings, a brave new world for me. I found quite serendipitously someone who would become my rehab specialist and my mentor. That entire process took about two years. My teaching studio then began to transform into something that called upon everything I had learned over my lifetime; from my upbringing and childhood experiences, to my post-secondary education and work experiences, to nearly thirty years as an occupational therapist in a multitude of roles in various departments and facilities, overlapping with forty years as a vocalist and bandleader in the performing and cultural arts sectors. I had a vision of what I wanted to create and how I wanted my studio to evolve.

Have I stopped? Never. I discovered ways to become even more resourceful. Every day I have new ideas and new projects. I find inspiration everywhere; every nook and cranny, every blog, every speech I hear, every person I meet, every authentic conversation I have with someone and every breath I take. I also seem to have found my way back to my sense of humour, which lately has surprised even me with its comedic value. Being told I am hilarious is a welcome relief from all the heavy introspection. Many have heard me say that the movie version of my life might be called, "Fifty Shades of OY."

The messages I want to give you to help you feel connected and supported are as follows:

One: Reclaim your voice

Find your anchor, your muse and a reason for living and staying alive. No matter how long it takes, or how painful it may be. Transformation and reinvention may seem daunting, but I truly believe that when you find and reclaim your "voice" you will find the way. I needed to completely revamp my career, my studio and my life, but could only achieve that by reclaiming my "why" and my "new voice." The connection between the physical, vocal and internal cannot be denied and may very well need healing. Learn strategies for speaking up and become your own Wonder Woman with your "Special Voice."

Two: Ask for help

When taking off the mask, ask for help. Find the one or two people you know who are unconditionally loving and supportive. Sometimes you may not know what you need so just talk it through, walk it through and cry as much as you need. Eventually, pieces of the puzzle will fall into place and you will regain your strength. I read somewhere that it is at our lowest points, when we feel the most broken, that in fact we are "broken open" and ready to realize, release and receive. Ask. Believe. Receive.

Three: Remember your self-care

That is vitally important. One foot in front of the other; get up and make your bed; put on some makeup if you wish; get dressed to go somewhere, anywhere, to a museum, a flower shop, a favourite store; treat yourself to a massage; go for a walk in nature; write down your thoughts in a journal; try a paint night; and remember your nutrition. Care for yourself.

Four: Acknowledge your accomplishments

Look back over your life and at all that you have accomplished and how far you have come. What brought you to this book and why are you reading it now? What do you need? Watch "It's a

Wonderful Life" many times over and realize the impact you have made on so many others. You cannot please or be everything to everyone. You have brilliance inside you and when you acknowledge your accomplishments, you release what no longer serves you, and "letting go of the past" will open the doors for new people, experiences and more positive energy.

Behind the mask was always that little girl longing to be a big girl who could make a difference, change the world for the better and do her own thing. The dream of being an international superstar performer, touring and recording artist was not meant to be for an eternity. The legacy transformed itself into combining the best of all I had known and learned over my lifetime to allow me to be the teacher, the muse, the role model and the inspirational mentor for the generations to follow. My credo has become "Changing Lives One Voice at a Time" and it is what I stand by and stand for. I do wish to leave you all with one last thought. The author is unknown, and this following affirmation has become a powerful force and reminder to me, so please take these words to heart in the manner and spirit with which they are offered. "Your life has purpose, your story is important, your dreams count, your voice matters and you were born to make an impact."

In blessed memory of my beloved late mother Mira.

About Florence

Florence Shustack is an accomplished, resourceful and courageous individual.

Born in Montreal and having graduated from McGill University with Distinction in 1977, Flo moved to Calgary in 1979. Her thirty years as an active occupational therapist in the areas of medical and mental health, special needs, rehabilitation, long-term care and administration have overlapped with forty years as vocalist, performer, bandleader, clinician, community theatre actress and creative musical consultant in the performing, educational and cultural arts sectors.

Flo has impacted many lives as well as having been impacted by many in return. Known for her motivational and inspirational personal stories, as well as her sense of humour, Flo's experiences and insights are empowering and transformative. As one notable local director put it, "Flo has, and is, a wealth of life experience, wisdom and professional knowledge."

Flo's Vocal Arts Studio has evolved over many decades becoming a multi-faceted, integrated and dimensional vocal performance studio, combining the best of Flo's professional therapy experience with her musical studies and performing arts career.

Inspiring her students and clients to live musically, passionately and courageously, while helping them reclaim and find their voices, has honoured her life's purpose. "Changing lives, one voice at a time," is her credo.

I AM a brilliant woman because I never gave up and I found ways to reclaim and embrace my voice.

— Florence Shustack

I AM Bold

I Was Born To Have Balls

By Brianna Hallet

Doris was one of the strongest women I knew. She had to fight to build her life. She began selling beauty products out of her trunk, with her toddler in tow. She built her business from one store into an empire of ten stores across the prairies. She was tough, spoke her mind and was hard-working. Doris was best friends with my boss, Ross. They were more like siblings. She supported him through his entire career as a salon owner, pushed him forward, had his back and even encouraged him to open a spa.

She also knew my secret: I was buying his business, SwizzleSticksSalonSpa.

Doris and I got to know each other very well on a trip though France. Between hectic train rides, Google Maps and lots of wine, we discussed the many ways that I could improve the business, from how I would be more inspirational to how fast I would relax the rigid rules. I remember her nodding, encouraging my youthful idealism. Little did I know that once both of my feet were on the other side, once anxiety attacks and sleepless nights became normal, I would discover what a genius she was for staying quiet.

Her most memorable saying was, "You don't know what you don't know." And I truly did not know! I didn't even know what I didn't know. I had no idea that during two years of going through the purchase agreement, my twelve-year relationship with Ryan would be tested over and over again. I didn't know that the hat I would wear most often would be for marketing and not for hairdressing or coaching the team. I didn't know that to be relevant and well known, I would have to be everywhere, at every event and on every social media platform. I didn't know that the deal would be the easy part. I bought a brand name that everyone knew. What I didn't know was what it would take to hold it up.

Doris knew.

The master plan preflight was beautiful. It was color-coded and mapped out perfectly. There were no scribbles and not a single wrinkle in the paper. Thing is, plans need to be lived in, adjusted, real.

Unfortunately, Doris passed away during my first year of ownership.

All too quickly she was diagnosed, had treatment and was gone. The industry had lost a magnate. She was a visionary, a cheerleader and as bold as a tiger.

And she left me with one hell of a gift. More than teaching me to speak less of things I didn't know, she left me a big set of balls. Literally. The kind one could hang off the hitch of a pickup truck. Ross gave them to me in the months following her passing and said, "Doris made me promise to give you these and she said, 'Grab some balls, honey, you're going to need them!'"

When we began negotiations for the deal, I, in my 27-year-old naivete, signed my very first Confidentiality Agreement. Always being adamant about following the rules, I felt this was like a giant weight. The only people at the time that knew about this plan were Ross, my angel investor and Ryan.

My suffering was in keeping it a secret. To get through to the other side of the business deal, I had to lie to some of my pillars, as I could no longer avoid them.

I had been managing the salon for about a year when we crafted the deal. It was our plan to get me used to being a boss, and to get the team adjusted to a new leader. 'Managing' was like driving my parents' car as a teen. I didn't own the car, but I could drive it, and even take it off road so long as I kept the gas tank full. It was easy to slide behind the wheel knowing if anything mechanical happened it really wasn't my issue. My team had respect for me, plus I was already softening some of the rigidity.

My sails were adjusted for the new winds. Three months into the deal, we celebrated Swizzmas, our annual Christmas party.

The party was held in the mountains, complete with a road trip and stunning vistas, and that was where the excitement ended. The sound system was horrid and the event was shaping up to be a dud.

I had some drinks and attempted to rile up some fun. The harder I tried, the more disengaged I became. I realized my identity had transformed. As much as I tried to revert to my old fun-loving, carefree self, I couldn't do it.

There is a fabulous TED Talk by Amy Cuddy. She speaks about how body language actually shapes who we are on a hormonal level. In the talk she states that in primate communities, when there is a change in alpha, the new leader goes through a very dramatic hormonal shift in a matter of days. The two significant hormones to shift are testosterone, which increases, and cortisol, which drops. This results in a powerful but calm leader.

My hormonal levels were already adjusted. To me, I wasn't just 'managing', I was at the helm of this ship and I had to pretend that I was only accompanying.

I ended up sneaking back to my room early that night. I just couldn't keep up the act. Ryan stayed out and had a really fun time. He returned to our room later to find me vegged out, braless, and playing Candy Crush. But at least I was real!

About a year into negotiations, I broke down and told my parents. The lying, hiding and skirting conversations were really starting to get to me. I was usually blunt, overly opinionated and would disagree just for a debate. This secret was forcing me to withdraw and be someone I was not. Keeping something from the ones I was most thankful for was changing who I was with them.

When I told them the big news, I distinctly remember underlining the words "confidentiality agreement." This deal was not to be shared with anyone. So, naturally, as proud parents do, they told everyone! Looking back on it now, I know they were really proud of their baby and wanted to shout it from the rooftops. But so did I dammit!

In the end, it took almost two years to close the deal. I was so tired of lying and holding my breath. I had gained a good fifteen pounds (I called it my *secret weight*). I was eating my truths instead of speaking them. Finally, the day came to reveal the truth to everyone. We told the master stylists and the next day the rest of the team. When Ross said that he sold the company, many people looked directly at me. As planned, they weren't shocked.

Was it all worth it?

YES!

The deal turned out to be the easy part. I finished signing on the dotted line just in time for the recession to hit and for a brand new government to be voted in. Business the only way I knew it had taken a dramatic turn. This was not in the master plan.

Having what felt like half of our target market laid off was a serious shift. I had bought at a premium and then had to fight for my life as we all watched the bottom fall out.

The first year was okay. The general population figured we would be back up before their severance packages ran out so spending continued without change for at least twelve months. Numbers declined, but money still flowed. I was coasting.

Darkness was coming and I truly did not know what I was going to do. After all, I had no business degree, no formal education and a debt larger than anyone I knew my age. On top of it all, we decided that Ryan should quit the job that was slowly emotionally killing him and instead study to become a financial advisor, the job that made his heart sing.

When life gets thick and unfriendly, for me it's about choice. Standing up and choosing the path, not letting the path choose me. I needed to feel in control and like I was meant to be there. So I dove head first into education. I hired a business coach, I joined the Chamber of Commerce, I engaged in networking events. Slowly, I started to learn what I needed to know--what I didn't know before.

In the further decline, my Board instructed me to cut 20% of costs. I was able to find savings simply by running lean. At the peak when I purchased, we spent a lot of money on the little things for convenience. It was necessary to trade that in for time spent. We slashed our marketing budget, we got rid of cleaners, and management took pay cuts. (Yes, I was now making even less than a top hairdresser with triple the workload… and no other stream of income.)

My attitude towards money is very effective. In truth, I believe that there is ALWAYS enough money! You may find yourself discovering some pretty amazing "recession wines" or hosting dinners instead of going out for them. There is always a way to do everything, you just need to keep flexible and feed your creativity.

If you are on the brink of something big, here are three success tips to get you started, or to push you over the top!

One: Smart Marketing

Your marketing direction needs to be thought out and turned upside down. You may find that those who benefit from adversity and change aren't at all who you have been targeting. Think carefully and creatively about what societal changes mean to your market. Is a new government pouring funding into the public sector? Maybe it's time to focus on teachers, nurses and students. Do you have a social enterprise? What community initiatives and non-profits are you supporting? Do you have an environmental position? Today's market wants to do good and they want their money to do good too! Be visible and choose excitement. But above all, remember that money isn't everything when it comes to advertising; it's really about the time you put in.

Two: Deal With it

Owning a business is multitasking, grinding it out and doing all of the unpleasantness. Converting all the strategy, mental space and thoughts that wake you up at night into something real is what it's all about.

You have to commit to being on 100% of the time. There are no breaks when you're reaching. You may have a teary meltdown behind the steering wheel on occasion. You may have days that you are not nice. You will have days that all you want to do is take your bra off and melt into the couch. But these sacrifices and changes make all the difference between surviving and thriving.

Three: Be Grateful

As hard as it may be to see the light and know that all of your hard work is paying off, it is important to think gratitude, sow humility and remember to be proud of yourself! Any anxiety and panic can always be tamed with gratitude. It is the one emotion that can slow you down and ground you at the same time.

My hope for you is that your beginning is a struggle and that you don't develop any bad habits or laziness. I hope that you learn what it's like to save a sinking ship. I hope you realize that lessons come in all forms, and may be learned years if not decades before you'll ever have a use for them. Energy and effort will always deliver. To be successful, an unwavering belief that you already are is essential.

And though my balls from Doris will forever live on the mantel in my home, Betty White said it perfectly: "Why do people say, 'Grow some balls?' Balls are weak and sensitive. If you want to be tough, grow a vagina. Those things can take a pounding."

About Brianna

Brianna Hallet is the Owner and CEO of SwizzleSticksSalonSpa located in the heart of Kensington Village, Calgary Alberta. Although she has owned the salon since 2014, she has been behind the chair at SwizzleSticks since 2007, and doing hair since 2000.

The kind of lessons learned at the beginning of owning a business are priceless, especially when the economy is in crisis. She believes that these lessons have made her a stronger entrepreneur today, and is grateful for the economic roller coaster she's been on since the sale. Since she has purchased the facility, she has undergone three major renovations. She has truly put her own mark on this landmark Calgary establishment.

SwizzleSticks is in its 30th year of business and what she believes keeps it successful and diverse is an intricate mixture that includes having the most amazing team, both on the floor and behind the scenes, and ensures that the guests always come first.

Leading the way in Environmental Stewardship, Swizz has had their very own bee hives since 2014, and will be adding a third hive this year! Swizz also recycles and diverts 90% of their waste by partnering with Green Circle Salons. Even the hair clippings are collected and made into oil booms!

SwizzleSticks dedicates over $100,000 in donations to local initiatives every year!

You can connect with Brianna at www.swizzlesticks.com

I AM a brilliant woman as I am resilient.

– Brianna Hallet

I AM Divine

The Rise to Fearless Freedom

By Tai-Monique Kristjansen

"When we deny our stories, they define us. When we own our stories, we get to write a brave new ending. Loving yourself through the process of your own story is the bravest thing you will ever do."

Brene Brown

Initially, my contribution for this book was not a story I anticipated sharing, ever! I've always known the Universe orchestrates opportunities and circumstances through people, places and events; so inevitably, the opportunity to write such a significant piece found its way to me.

When Karen invited me to contribute my story for her upcoming book, I anticipated with excitement about the type of anecdote she had in mind for me to present until I read the topic in her email. Suddenly I was flooded with a vast wave of chills that flushed straight through my heart and sunk down to my womb. As my throat constricted, I felt faint. Karen's proposed book struck a debilitating fear into me. I intuitively knew precisely what was being offered: an opportunity that would allow me to make peace with an experience that had been keeping my soul hostage, holding me in a suspended state of silent suffering.

As the days and nights passed, the more restless and deeply anxious I became. Late one sleepless night, I prayed to God asking for divine guidance, to show me three distinct signs that writing this chapter was the path intended to serve my highest good.

Immediately, I was guided to do a spread with my oracle cards, which revealed "Come Out Of The Closet," "You Are Seeing The Situation Clearly," "Trust" and "Fertility."

The following day, on Facebook, my newsfeed was flooded with countless women—some of whom were my dearest friends—from all over the world sharing their shocking and painful experiences of being sexually victimized as part of the MeToo Movement.

I found the courage to share my story with my weekly Trilotherapy group as we were asked to do mirror work exercises the previous week and share our experiences. After I spoke, I felt completely held in a safe container of love, understanding and tremendous support. I now knew within my heart that the synchronicities were evident. The Universe was reflecting back to me what was no longer serving me and speaking loud and clear in my ear, "It's time to step through fear and into freedom beloved, speak your truth, share your story and step into the light..." Those three signs within three days came to fruition.

For fifteen years, I pursued a career in the film and entertainment industry as a professional dancer, model, actor, stunt double, DJ and creative artist. While overseas on one of my contracts, I was drugged and raped. #MeToo.

Such an excruciating and traumatizing experience left me feeling petrified, ashamed and utterly alone. I was plagued by nightmares and flashbacks that rocked me to the root of my soul. I completely lost my mind; every fiber of my being was filled with fire and rage. My body had been severely violated; I was emotionally bruised and broken. The purity of my essence was shattered. In my state of shock I completely shut myself down into silence.

When I had to leave the house, engage in a casual conversation or attempt to formulate coherent thoughts, these simple and normal acts were at times beyond my ability. It was as if an unknown entity had forced its way in, stolen my spirit and smothered my light.

My vision for the future became undetermined. I lost my sense of direction of where to go or what to do next. Wherever I went, I felt overexposed, as if everyone knew just by looking at me that I had been raped. The shame and humiliation was overwhelming. As a coping mechanism, I intoxicated myself with alcohol, numbed myself with substances and took risks with my finances. Everything in my entire life that I had worked so hard to build and achieve began to slip out of my grip. I started to lose touch with who I was; drifting away, barely existing and ultimately falling apart.

I was so infuriated with God one night that I cried out my rage so loud it could have reached the heavens. Filled with anger and resentment, I pleaded and demanded answers as to why did this ever happen to me. All that echoed back was a profound silence. Within the stillness, I suddenly knew this experience was meant to serve my greater purpose. I cried myself to sleep in the presence of the *dark night of the soul.*

The next day, God sent me an earth angel in the form of a new friend to help me through my grieving process. He opened up his home next to the ocean and held space for me as I crumbled deep into my darkness, welcoming the depths of my depression. With his unconditional love, support and unwavering faith in me, I began to regain my trust in humanity. He was my shining light that helped me see through the shadows of despair. I will forever be in gratitude to him as his divine grace helped save my life.

It was crystal clear to me that the time had come to step away from living a passionate lifestyle and into fulfilling my purpose. Still overseas and six weeks after the incident, I took a leap of faith and forged an entrepreneurial relationship with a skincare, health and wellness company and began building my international business.

Several months later, I auditioned for another dance company and trained with a troupe full-time with the opportunity to re-launch my dance career. I immersed myself in learning a beauty and fashion curriculum to compliment my new pursuits. There were still days, even weeks, where I felt paralyzed to get out of bed and face the new opportunities that were blossoming. Soon, depression had claimed me again and I was forced to surrender. My dear friend and business partner advised me to seek help from a NLP (Neuro Linguistic Programing) coach. During one of our intense sessions he interrupted to ask me, "Why are you still trying to pursue a life here – in a foreign country, faced daily with your trauma, far away from your family and solid support system?" It was my light bulb moment.

I moved back to Canada to be with my family and reconnect with my roots. I enhanced my yoga practice and meditations, determined to rise and persevere. Still reeling from the trauma, I spent quality time reading, writing, reflecting and contemplating. "What was the higher purpose of this experience?" "What is it ultimately showing and teaching me?" My questions kept resurfacing.

I came across a book in my sister's library, Radical Forgiveness by Colin C. Tipping, and dove right in. His philosophy on forgiveness spoke to my soul and expanded my awareness on our "sacred contracts." Our purpose is to learn life lessons and help others navigate towards a spiritual evolution as we collectively raise consciousness. Prior to our time here, we create agreements with other souls to help fulfill our sacred contracts. I came to the realization that my experience happened to me through divine order, precisely as planned to further my spiritual growth and development. This was the pivotal point in my sacred healing journey. In fully accepting and owning my circumstances, I became rooted in the understanding that it was my purpose to come into a holistic space of unconditional love, forgiveness, compassion and humility. I was the only one with the key to unlock this universal truth –forgive my attacker and break through the restraint to heal myself – believe in my strength and resilience to pursue my self worth and find my inner peace. The more I surrendered to spirit, the more I emerged into a new space of faith, trust, liberation and freedom.

In my daily meditations, I made powerful intentions to live more of my soul's purpose. This inspired the decision to move back into my apartment in Vancouver. Whilst on a visit making arrangements, Wayne Dyer had passed. It deeply saddened me. I had the great honour of attending one of his live talks, which was a magical and unforgettable experience. When I listened to Wayne's teachings on my travels I always felt grounded by his inspirational wisdom.

As I was formulating the final details of my exit move, a friend invited me to an event in Edmonton that was being held in his honour. I felt compelled to attend given my great admiration for this spiritual leader and his life's work.

As soon as I walked in to the room, a sudden familiarity washed over me. Everything Matt, the facilitator, spoke about resonated so deep that it ignited a spark within me. I envisioned and received many intuitive messages that night and within two days, I was hired for a position that aligned perfectly with my international business venture. This was the deciding factor for me to remain in Edmonton.

I had met Matt at the event and we continued to connect. The more we did, the more I realised we were vibrating on the same frequency. He offered to give me a Reiki healing session, and even though I'd previously studied Reiki overseas, I'd completely forgotten about this healing phenomenon. Our enlightening experience was so powerful for the both of us that I felt my fiery spirit slip back into my body and I knew I was home. In that moment, we both understood that our purpose in this lifetime together was to teach others how to heal themselves, help humanity move forward and assist in raising the vibration of consciousness.

In less than four months of knowing each other, we started an intimate relationship and moved in together. Weeks later, we then launched our healing practice Sacred Awakenings on

Valentine's Day. Shortly after, I was introduced to a self-love and forgiveness coach, Jeri Tourand, who introduced me to Zen Trilotherapy. These ancient Buddhist teachings combined with Western psychology gave me the tools to fine-tune my inner engineering and wholeheartedly heal my trauma. I came to realize you have to take your deepest wound and make it your greatest power. And through the power of this work, I found the gift in healing myself to pursue my practice further to support other women and men who have suffered similar circumstances and to be a voice for those who continue to suffer in silence. For this experience I am so grateful, as it has led me on the path to awaken more of my inner brilliance and ultimately fulfill my sacred contract.

When a woman steps into her power she shines her light and invites other women and men to do the same. I now invite you to do the same. This is an empowering time for the feminine force within you to rise up as there is a vast awakening in consciousness that is dismantling the old patriarchal paradigms. It is creating a realm of transcendental love to emerge. This spiritual rebalancing with the powerful rise of the Divine Feminine in harmony with the Divine Masculine spirit moves the human race forward, elevates our spiritual consciousness, heals our ancestral past and guides us on our evolutionary path towards freedom.

"So too as the lotus flower, we have the ability to rise from the mud, out of the darkness and into the light. Heartbreak, pain, conflict and imperfection are opportunities to emerge from the concealed depths to the gleaming luminescence and become stronger. It is your choice to decide whether to drown in your troubles or courageously survive. We can overcome our obstacles on our journey towards enlightenment and flourish. As deeper the mud, the more beautiful the Lotus blooms."

– Unknown Author

I AM a brilliant woman.

About Tai-Monique

Tai-Monique is an enthusiastic lifestyle entrepreneur who is creating a "life by design," living her highest excitements and fulfilling her divine purpose. Co-founder of Sacred Awakenings, Tai-Monique is an Usui and Karuna Reiki Master, an Intuitive Crystal, Sound and Energy Healer and educator, as well as a Numerologist, Zen Trilotherapy and Life Coach. She strongly believes in the future of our next generation and teaches children Meditation practices and Reiki. Additionally, she works with the Spiritually-Gifted Youth.

As a speaker and international multi-business owner, she drives a team of aspiring leaders to help transform the lives of others while fulfilling their own pursuits and dreams of extraordinary choice. Passionate about service and leadership, Tai-Monique is constantly involved in various projects, particularly those that support women in their efforts to reclaim a sacred sovereignty and divine feminine wisdom with a view to live an inspired, spirit-filled, enriched life of authenticity, self-love, joy and freedom.

Together with her life partner, Matt Welke, and their beautiful dog, Gandalf, they are on an accelerated mission with a grand vision to help people re-awaken to their true sacred selves, to live in a world filled with more love, peace, equality and unity.

For healing sessions, workshops, training and certification, personal coaching or speaking engagements, please visit Tai-Monique at www.sacred-awakenings.com

I AM a brilliant woman who inspires other brilliant women to stand in their light, own their truth and reclaim their power.

— Tai-Monique Kristjansen

About Women Embracing Brilliance

Women Embracing Brilliance was created to support, encourage and celebrate women who are committed to expressing their voice, reclaiming their feminine power and embracing the highest version of who they are – *their Brilliant Self.*

Our vision over the next five years is to positively impact the lives of women around the world by empowering them to embrace and stand in their boldness, brilliance and beauty.

How? When one woman embraces her brilliance, her *soul signature* radiates out through her own voice of love, compassion and encouragement, which plants a seed in those around her. That seed becomes a ripple effect igniting the light within others and contributing to the evolution of humanity.

We are a global community of heart centered women who are dedicated to making a difference by empowering each other to live in optimal health, love and prosperity. As we embrace and ignite our brilliance we create heaven on earth for all.

Visit us at <u>www.womenembracingbrilliance.com</u>

If you have a story that you are ready to share, and would love to be a contributing author in Volume Four of:

I AM a Brilliant Woman contact Karen Klassen

<u>karen@karenklassen.ca</u>

97135036R00088

Made in the USA
Columbia, SC
14 June 2018